Enamelling

Enamelling

Joan Bolton King

The Art of Crafts

First published in 2001 by
The Crowood Press
Ramsbury, Marlborough
Wiltshire, SN8 2HR

British Library Cataloguing-in-Publication Data
A catalogue record for this book is available from the British Library.

ISBN 1 86126 437 2

Dedication
This book is dedicated to the members of the Guild of Enamellers, through whom I learned much of my craft gained and an unending enthusiasm for the art of enamelling.

Illustration Acknowledgements
Twenty major photographs of the author's finished pieces were taken by Behram Kapadia; the majority of the remainder where taken by the author. The kingfisher brooch decorating the chapter titles is by Gerald Lomax.

Line illustrations on pages 51, 70, and 78 by the author; all other line illustrations by Keith Field.

Acknowledgements
I am indebted to those enamellers who readily gave me photographs of their work for inclusion in this book, to Emma Hughes and Barbara Wigglesworth for some of the secondary photographs, and especially to Behram Kapadia for his advice and the professionalism of his pictures.

A number of members of the Guild of Enamellers have my sincere gratitude for their help in compiling this book, especially Maureen Astle, who painstakingly advised and checked the text as the book has taken shape.

Publisher's Note
The author and publisher have made every effort to ensure that the instructions in this book are safe and accurate, and therefore cannot accept any liability for any injury, damage or loss to persons or property, however they may occur.

Designed and typeset by Annette Findlay

Printed and bound in Singapore by Craft Print International Ltd.

Contents

1 Introduction

Enamelling is the fusing of glass to metal: the two permanently bond together when heated until the glass actually melts. For practical purposes, in modern creative enamelling the glass is usually of a high jewellery grade and the metal is copper or silver; although gold, stainless steel or other metals may be used for more specialized purposes.

A wide range of colours are produced by adding various oxides during the manufacture of the enamel. Each of these is produced in both transparent and opaque forms. Transparent enamel provides a thin translucent coat through which the metal, or an underlying enamel, can be seen; while an opaque enamel gives a dense glaze, covering everything beneath it. Very fine and highly pigmented enamels can also be used for painting.

Nowadays the term 'enamel' is used for an enamelled piece as well as the specially prepared glass (also known as enamel) used to enamel it. This vitreous enamel should not be confused with those far less durable domestic 'enamel paints', so called after their enamel-like shiny finish, or the modern plastic- or resin-coated enamel-style trinkets that mimic the colourful glories of true enamelling with various degrees of success.

THE HISTORY AND DEVELOPMENT OF ENAMELLING

Enamelling is a very ancient craft, dating at least from the twelfth century BC. Some of the earliest examples were in the cloisonné technique, where gold wires were embedded in enamel to form a design composed of cells, into which glass of various colours was fused. These date back to the Mycenaean empire and some can still be seen in the Nicosia Museum in Cyprus.

The craft spread slowly and spasmodically through Mediterranean countries and the Romans later took it right to the Celtic fringes of their empire (including Britain). These early craftsmen developed the technique of champlevé, where the enamel is inlaid into recesses dug out of the metal, and in the Byzantine period this was frequently used to produce large religious artefacts, often of gilded copper. The steady advance in craftsmanship and equipment gave rise to new techniques and to an expansion of the range of objects enamelled. By the twelfth century France, and Limoges in particular, had become the primary centre of excellence.

Exquisite coloured enamelled pictures began to be painted in the fifteenth century and developed alongside the monochrome art of grisaille, where layers of semi-opaque white enamel are painted over a dark background. In the mid-eighteenth century English artist enamellers invented a way to reproduce high-quality pictures using transfer printing, thereby cutting costs and so creating new markets for these enamels.

The early enamellers experienced great difficulty in obtaining clear and consistent colours, and in firing their work in primitive kilns. Techniques improved but it remained a chancy business. In 1721, J.-P. Ferrand published a marvellously illustrated treatise, *L'Art du Feu*. This classic work contained very practical instructions on how to master the craft; however, it also included topical astrological advice such as to remember the influence of Saturn on lead (then an integral part of all glass) and only to work with this element on Saturdays!

Many highly desirable enamels were produced throughout the world during the last two centuries. European enamellers prospered, among them the Russian jeweller and goldsmith Carl Fabergé, who incorporated enamels of remarkable translucence in his work and is best known for the priceless series of 'Imperial Easter Eggs'. The Chinese, meanwhile, had perfected their robust style of cloisonné, having imported the necessary skills from the West some five hundred years earlier, and the art of enamelling became relatively common in the Middle and Far East. More recently, enamellers from the Americas and Australia have become very skilful and now often take a lead in embracing modern artistic trends. Fine examples of enamels can be seen in most leading museums, such as London's British Museum and Victoria and Albert Museum.

The best enamellers of today have continued the tradition of producing work of the highest quality and most top enamellers now use very sophisticated computerized kilns. However, a phenomenal expansion of the craft took place after the Second World War, following the development of efficient and small electric and gas kilns that made enamelling accessible to anyone who wanted to practise it in their own home. Since then amateurs and professionals alike have enamelled, experimented and introduced artistry in their own inimitable ways.

THE SCOPE OF THIS BOOK

This book covers the basic principals of enamelling in such a way that the beginner can enjoy its delights right from the moment they get going. It shows how a budding enameller (an 'enamellist' to the Americans) could set up and start working, initially using simple techniques. Skills, and an increasing knowledge of the craft, will be learned by working through the projects in the first part so that a new enameller can go on to try out any of the more advanced techniques explained in the later chapters.

Most of the enamelling is done on copper; it is an inexpensive metal, ideal for learning the craft and in itself the perfect base for many of the more sophisticated techniques. The book is intended for

'Watchful Kingfisher', worked in ordinary and liquid enamels.

someone enamelling at home and stops short of demanding the use of workshop tools or a specialized knowledge of the arts of the engraver or silversmith. However, those who may ultimately want to go on to enamel in these ways will have acquired some knowledge of what is involved and an excellent grounding in the art. Examples of finished pieces in the more advanced techniques are pictured in the Gallery.

The inclusion of many practical and economical tips should enable anyone to successfully follow the instructions. They are particularly designed to help those taking up enamelling without the help of formal tuition, but they should also provide established enamellers with plenty of new ideas. Suggestions are given to encourage individual enamellers to explore the artistry of this unusual craft.

I hope that this book will provide the reader with an enthralling and rewarding new interest, and some of the absorbing pleasure that I have gained from enamelling.

2 How to Start Up

LOCATION

Craft or hobby enamelling can be done in a designated workspace, such as a spare room, or on the kitchen table, with the equipment easily packed away afterwards. Good ventilation and a convenient electric power point are necessary, and you need easy access to running water for several techniques. There are also safety considerations in choosing the best location and it is a good idea to have your working area at least a few feet away from the kiln.

THE KILN

Most enamel work is small and, unless you are planning on producing larger pieces, an electric U5 (alternatively TK191) or EF110 kiln will suffice. They are powered at under 1kw and are less than 1ft (25cm) cubic size, but have a firing chamber that will take something up to 4in (10cm) across. The little gas kilns are only suitable for very small pieces and may be hard to obtain. Well-kept kilns are usually easily sold second-hand, should you want something bigger

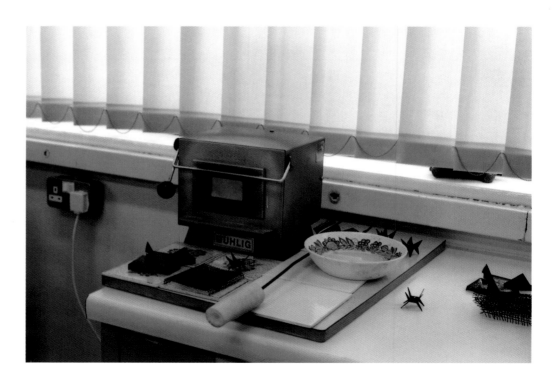

A kiln in place.

Tools normally included with beginner's kits.

later on. Old-fashioned hood kilns or blowtorches are not considered here for safety reasons.

HOW COSTLY?

Most people are surprised by how relatively inexpensive it is to start enamelling, especially if you deduct what you have avoided spending on buying presents by giving away your new creations. The kiln is the major outlay, but is a one-off expense and therefore should be chosen carefully. Using copper instead of precious metals such as gold and silver also keeps the cost down.

Kilns can be bought from the enamel suppliers listed at the back of the book, but buying an inclusive beginner's or starter's kit may be the best course. All the suppliers will send catalogues if requested, but do check whether their prices include VAT: most do not.

As well as a kiln these kits contain the essential tools: a firing fork; a metal mesh and stilt for putting the enamel into the kiln; an abrasive sponge; a sifter (a small sieve or tea strainer); and a palette knife and tweezers for preparing the piece. In addition most include a hooked swirling tool for manipulating the molten glass. To this list I suggest you add: a second stilt, so you have a small and a large one; a medium carborundum stone; and a half-round needle file (obtainable from hardware shops).

Kits also include a small selection of enamels (opaque and/or transparent powder), some decorative mediums (solid bits) and a few assorted pieces of copper. You will soon exhaust some of these supplies, so it may be a good idea to select some additional items at the same time as ordering a kiln or kit. If you want to follow the ideas in this book, you will need ten each of circles about 1in (2.5cm) across and ovals 1½in (4cm) long. Also choose some of the small fancy copper blanks that appeal to you, such as tortoise, teddy bear, flower or star – sized 1–1½in (2.5–4cm) – and with a hole for fitting chains, etc. ('P' numbers show they are pierced.) Those who learn quickly

Safety

Kilns
Kilns are designed to be safe on a table or work surface, but I like to place mine on a piece of chipboard big enough to have at least a couple of ordinary ceramic wall tiles glued onto it in front of the kiln and ready to take the hot pieces. The vital thing is to remember that the inside of the kiln will get red hot and so will everything that has been in it. Should you accidentally burn yourself, hold the affected part under cold running water for up to ten minutes until it stops stinging. Prompt medical advice should always be sought for serious burns.

Lead
The second important safety consideration is that the enamel itself can be toxic, with many enamels containing some lead. This is an integral part of the majority of glasses and normally no danger; however, when ground into grains or a powder, special care is needed to make sure it is never swallowed or inhaled. Keep it right away from food and drink, avoid smoking while enamelling and always wash your hands thoroughly afterwards. (Needless to say, biting one's nails and enamelling do not mix safely!)

Good ventilation is necessary around any kiln, particularly those heated by gas, and this can add to one's comfort on a hot day. It is also essential if you want to use acids (*see* page 30).

Finally, although a more remote risk, never stare too long into a red hot kiln.

A twin stilt and other suggested additional tools.

will soon progress to dishes and I suggest they get two or three shallow round ones each of 2½in and 3½in (6.5cm and 9cm).

You may like to supplement the enamels in the kit with small quantities (probably 2oz, or 50g) of a few more of the cheaper opaque colours that you like; also some soft white and possibly some more ordinary black and white. Miniature jam jars make good containers for enamels supplied in plastic bags.

All this will give you a good basic stock, but if you have not got the exact item I suggest later, then substitute something you possess. This will also help you to develop an individual style in your enamelling and by the time you need to order more you will have a far better idea of what you personally like.

3 Starting with the Basics

There are several basic methods of applying enamel to a metal base and countless ways of achieving the desired ornamentation. This part of the book is designed to give you a sound knowledge of how to enamel simple pieces, and an understanding of the underlying principles. It includes detailed methods for using the enamel in various ways with advice to help you succeed, and it is strongly recommended that the budding enameller try out all the initial series of 'Mini-Projects'. Each introduces a different basic technique, all of which can be combined later.

Copper blanks, sold in regular shapes and popular novelty designs, are ideal for the beginner and will be used, in the first place, with opaque colours only; transparent colours will be explored later.

Turn the kiln on in time to give it at least half an hour to heat before it is needed. Also, put a shallow bowl of cold water beside it for use later.

A novice's owl key ring.

Mini-Project – Enamelling a Simple Blank

The enamelling method of sprinkling the powdery grains of coloured glass onto the copper involves twelve stages; it can then be referred to again and again until it is second nature. For this project, blue is used on a small copper disk.

A copper blank before (left) and after enamelling.

1. Clean one side of the blank; you need to remove any dirt from one surface if the glass is to fuse to the metal. Rubbing it with the abrasive sponge is the easiest way but, alternatively, it can be scrubbed with whatever you use to clean your saucepans. Take care not to leave any trace of grease, and avoid letting sticky fingers touch the cleaned copper.
2. Prepare a clean space. Work on some shiny paper, wiped clean of dust, especially any bits from the sponge (keep a piece of lint-free cloth or an old handkerchief for this). Enamel

Cleaning with an abrasive sponge.

U5 kiln's maximum temperature of about 900°C. A mesh or stilt is used to lift the piece into the kiln with a firing fork; the palette knife and tweezers will be needed to pick it off the paper.

5. Place the piece on the mesh. Carefully slide the palette knife underneath the enamel-covered piece, while stopping it moving by placing the points of the tweezers on the paper opposite the knife, then lift the piece, taking care not to disturb the enamel on top. It is then a good idea to put the tweezers down and place the covered blank onto the slightly curved palm and fingers of the left hand (assuming you are right-handed). The knife is then withdrawn and cleaned before being used to place the piece gently onto the mesh.

powder is precious and must never get contaminated, so you can tip whatever falls round the blank back into the pot. All of your equipment must also be kept clean.

3. Sift on your colour; a fine-mesh tea strainer is commonly used for this. Pour some enamel into it, then practice spreading an even coat by tapping it gently while keeping it moving slowly over the area to be covered. When you can achieve a level coating try it over the cleaned side of the blank until you cannot see any copper showing through. If the powder falling onto the paper around the edges of the blank looks thin, you can be pretty sure that it will need a little more on the copper in that area. Edges must always be well covered.

4. Get your tools ready. By now the kiln should be getting up to 800–850°C. You can estimate the temperature by the colour of the firing chamber. At a dull red it is not really hot enough: wait until it starts to glow, even turning a bright pale orange as it reaches a

Lifting the piece.

A pallet knife being withdrawn for cleaning.

Sifting on the enamel.

6. Put the piece in the kiln. Practice using the firing fork to lift the mesh, keeping it level, then gently putting it down again. Remember the kiln is now very hot, as will be anything that has been in it, however briefly. Should you find the doorknob uncomfortably hot, hold it in a fold of cloth without letting the material touch the side of the kiln. When you open the kiln door try to avoid losing too much heat: shut it again as soon as possible. On the other hand, do not rush things so much that you jog the piece and spill enamel on the kiln floor: carefully place the piece in the kiln and quickly, but softly, close the door.

7. Fire the piece to fuse the glass with the metal. A small piece very soon heats in the kiln, and once it approaches the melting point of the enamel things happen very rapidly. The grains often darken, then look 'sugary' while they fuse, and quickly join together as they acquire a shiny surface, still with a slightly lumpy look. The enamel has now fused to the copper. (You can often see through the mica window of a new kiln, but this inevitably clouds over with use.) This initial lumpy 'orange peel' look soon smoothes out, but if the piece is left in the kiln too long the edges will burn out, as will places where the powder has been applied too thinly. For simple enamels it is often best to take them out at the 'orange peel' stage in all but the final firing.

All this takes a minute or two at most, but the actual time varies because of three factors: the nature of the enamel, the heat of the kiln and the mass of cold substances you are putting in it. Therefore it is not possible to give precise timings. With practice you will soon learn to catch it at the right moment, but try to avoid opening the door too often to have a peep, allowing the firing chamber to cool excessively.

Placing the mesh in a hot kiln.

8. Cool the piece and clean it. Place the mesh with your fired piece on a fireproof surface to cool (such as the tile in front of the kiln, if you have one) and be careful to avoid burning yourself or the table top. After a short time it will be safe to pick the piece up with the tweezers and touch the edge into the water; however, if it gives out a loud hiss, it is still too hot and immersing it would shatter or crack the glass. After a few moments more it can be slowly cooled, continually touching the water until it makes no further noise, and it may then be safely be dropped into the dish. Before you go any further pour the excess enamel back into the pot, wipe the paper and clean your tools.

Firescale on the back of the fired piece.

Testing to see if it is cool enough to immerse in water.

9. Dry the enamelled disk. Black copper oxide will have formed on its exposed back: this is 'firescale' and must not be allowed to contaminate the enamel. Much of it will probably have come off in the water, but any other bits that might possibly flake off should be removed before you take it back to the clean working area; use a bit of fine sand or emery paper or, better still, some wet and dry paper.

10. 'Counter-enamel' the piece, that is, put another coat of enamel on the back. This counteracts the stresses that build up between the copper and the enamel as it heats or cools: otherwise there is a risk of bits 'pinging off' the copper; also, enamelling both sides reduce the risk of warping. Counter-enamel need not be your best enamel, and a cheap enamel is often sold for this purpose.

Note that the copper does not need further cleaning, as any dirt on the reverse will have burnt off and the little remaining copper oxide firescale is assimilated and disappears in the fusing with the covering coat of opaque enamel.

When enamelling the second side the piece cannot be placed on a mesh without sticking to it, so a stilt has to be used to hold it up, just by its edges. Small stilts can be placed on a mesh, and large ones are usually shaped to take the firing fork.

Repeat stages 2–8 with the counter-enamel.

Sometimes the enamel on the back of the piece will cause it to stick to the stilt. Free it by holding the piece with the tweezers and firmly tapping the stilt on the tile. However, this may

Counter-enamelled piece being placed on a small stilt.

leave a stilt mark, which can have very sharp edges that must be stoned back immediately.
11. Improve the appearance of the first side by adding a second top coat, repeating stages 2–8 and using a stilt.
12. Finally finish the piece by stoning or filing off any rough places and cleaning the firescale off the edges of the copper (holding the stone at right angles to the enamelled surface).

Your first enamel is something to be proud of and should be kept for use later. You should also now have a useful knowledge of the basic principles of enamelling and be able to go straight on to making really attractive simple items.

A SELECTION OF FINDINGS

The next series of mini-projects will show a variety of easy ways of enamelling pieces that can be converted into something useful by attaching a 'finding'. Some are fixed through a hole pierced in the copper, others glued on the back. Copper blanks can be bought without a hole – one can be drilled or punched through the copper – or they are acquired with one already there (catalogued 'P'). A hole cannot be added to an already enamelled piece, although it can be filled and enamelled over.

Fridge magnets and brooch pins are best glued on with an epoxy glue (the sort that comes in two tubes) or, failing that, a superglue. Roughen the counter-enamel

TIPS

- Placing the sifter down on the paper when tipping in the enamel stops it falling straight through.
- The fork's prongs should not be allowed to protrude beyond the mesh so the piece can be placed right at the back of the kiln.
- Giving an empty sifter a tap on the table leg will clear out any residual enamel.
- Always check a newly fired piece and its stilt for any sharp projections.
- The back of the kiln is the hottest part – use it whenever possible.

Stoning the edge.

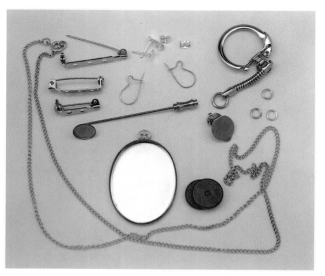

A selection of findings.

to give the glue something to bite onto and choose the biggest pin you have that will be hidden behind the piece.

Pendant chains are attached using a jump ring, and key rings usually come with a strong integral ring. It is a good idea to use only silver or silver-plated ear studs or wires to avoid any allergic reaction.

Remember that key rings are liable to receive rough treatment in a pocket, so only fit them to sturdy enamelled shapes that are unlikely to get bent. Also bear in mind that enamelling makes earrings heavy.

ENAMELS – PLAIN AND DECORATIVE FORMS

Suppliers' catalogues offer a bewildering choice of enamels. Most are sold in powdered (granular) form and these are divided into opaque or transparent colours. For simplicity we are currently working with the opaques, but transparents will be introduced in Chapter 5. You could consider buying sample sets in order to try differently coloured enamels.

A selection of decorative media.

The enamels themselves can be bought in lump form or in geometric shapes, designed for decorative purposes and usually listed as 'decorative media'. Most kits include an assortment, and the following mini-projects give suggestions on how to use some of the more common forms.

Mini-Project – A Millefiori on a Star

Millefiori are multi-coloured glass beads, like a cross-section from a stick of 'rock' sweet, that can be fired into the enamel. In the photograph below an orange one has been chosen to complement the yellow background.

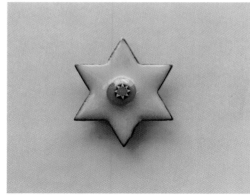

Millefiori bead melted onto a star.

1. Clean the copper star (or a flower or circle) and enamel the front and back with one coat each (points 1–10 of the 12-point programme).
2. The second coloured coat is sprinkled on, the piece put on the stilt and the millefiori bead is very carefully placed centrally on top of the layer of powder with the tweezers. If you are

not satisfied with the position it can be delicately moved sideways so it 'skates' into place over the surface of the powdered enamel; then, with a pencil or tool, push it downwards so it settles firmly into the powdered coat. In this way you can ensure it is safely positioned; however, if you have dragged or pushed it through the grains so it leaves the smooth first coat exposed it will probably move during firing and you had best re-sprinkle and try again.

An owl with two small millefiori eyes before final firing on a twin stilt.

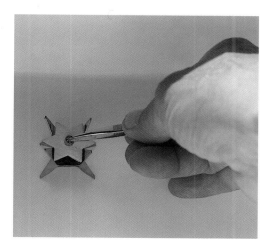

Millefiori being settled into the second coat.

3. With the bead and powder on the stilt it is ready to fire, but be careful not to jolt it as you place it in the kiln or close the door. The powdered glass will melt before the bead and the piece should be left until the millefiori has just become mushroom-shaped, but before the edge of the enamel begins to burn out, leaving a black line. With a large bead and some delicate enamels the best timing will require some compromises.
4. Cool the piece, clean the edges and fit a finding.

Mini-Project – Tortoise and Chips

These chips are just small chippings of lump enamel, intended to fuse together when fired. Opaque or transparent chips can be used with varying effects.

Tortoise enamelled with a shell of fused chips.

1. Enamel the front twice and back once (points 1–11 of the 12-point list). The tortoise 'shell' needs to be covered with the chipped bits of enamel, and this time a little glue will be needed to keep them from falling off.

Improving your Twin Stilt

Finding the best way to support different small shapes on a stilt becomes easier if you use pliers to widen out the four arms on one side of a twin stilt. This gives you the choice of two alternative sizes.

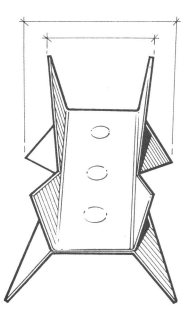

Twin stilt with the arms on one side spread wide.

Glue for enamelling must be able to burn out without trace and proprietary brands are obtainable; however you can make your own by mixing a thin, but really sticky, solution of the granular form of commercial wallpaper paste, in pure water.

Enamelled blank fired to 'orange peel', and the selected chips.

2. Select some small coloured bits from the mixed chips, wet the top of the tortoise body with enamelling gum and place the bits carefully up to the edge, but not over it. They will spread out as they melt, so take particular care not to cover the hole, if it is wanted. A minute chip will make an appropriate eye.

   Leave the glue enough time to dry completely – the piece will now be easier to move, but even more importantly, if any wet glue had been left it would boil when put in the kiln and you can imagine how this would propel any adjacent chips! Care is always needed not to spill enamel, powder or lump, onto the floor of the kiln.

3. Fire until the shell looks smooth and shiny, finish and then fit the finding.

Tortoise, piled with chips on its stilt, ready to fire.

DOMED SHAPES AND SHALLOW DISHES

These can usually be enamelled by sprinkling, without any glue, but if the sides are too steep for the enamel to stay in place, then spread the glue reasonably sparingly with a brush or finger (be careful not to miss anywhere) and quickly sprinkle on the enamel while the glue is still wet. An even covering is needed all over the curved surface of the dish, and this is best achieved by picking up the piece and holding it at different angles so the powder always falls at right angles to the surface being covered. Shake any enamel off your hands and wash them.

Gum being spread with a finger.

Curved surface in optimum position for sprinkling.

When the piece is fired concave side up, it is often hard to avoid the stilt leaving marks on any already enamelled surface underneath, but marking its top can be avoided if the underneath of a domed blank is counter-enamelled first. For a dish, where the inside is the most important side, complete this before the piece is finally turned over to finish counter-enamelling the convex underside. Backs of dishes usually need more than one coat of counter-enamel.

Remember that firescale will form on exposed copper every time it is fired. Ways to get rid of this will be explained in the next chapter (*see* page 30), but in the meantime just make sure you always remove all bits that could flake off with the sand/emery paper, and keep those black bits right away from your working area.

TIPS

- Home-made mixed 'wallpaper' gum can be saved in a bottle for some days.
- Should your gluing and sprinkling go wrong and need to be wiped off, the enamel can be dried and reused.

Mini-Project – Domed Oval with Random Mosaic

Small lumps of any pale colour can be used on a dark background. It might be as well to re-read through the 12-point programme again to remind yourself of the basic information as well as the recommended processes.

Mosaic formed by melting pale blue pieces into a black background enamel.

1. First counter-enamel the back, firing it on the mesh, before you put on the two top coats, and always remember that the enamel will recede from the edges unless they are generously covered. The slight curve in the copper should present no problem, so use the usual methods without glue and, while choosing a suitable stilt for the oval shape, note how much less contact there is when it is positioned with its domed side up.
2. Give the blank a third sprinkling of the black to ensure a really dense colouring, and put it on the stilt.
3. Select some small opaque lumps or medium-sized chippings and gently place them individually on the piece, leaving a gap between them, so as to allow them to spread on melting.

Pieces being positioned prior to firing.

Pattern of decorative media fired into a dish.

Also, do not put them right up to the edge because the doming makes them far more liable to fall off the outer area.

There is an alternative method for anyone with a really unsteady hand: fire the third black coat, then glue the pieces on before re-firing. However, this will probably leave a more lumpy final effect.

4. Fire the lumps into the third coat, finish off the piece and fit a finding.

PROJECT – MOSAIC PATTERN DISH

It is time to try something more ambitious on one of the small shallow dishes, using what has been learned already.

1. Decide on the background colour and a selection of decorative media that can be placed centrally to form the design. If one piece is put in the middle, others can be arranged round it in a regular manner, and this can be tried out experimentally in the copper dish. Beware of being too lavish with the pieces and consider various shapes: mosaics (round, square or octagonal), small millefiori, beads, threads, or any others you have. Try to avoid having too much to be melted in the middle of the dish as this could easily just form a molten lake if fired for too long. Make a note of your design so you can relay it later.

2. Enamel the inside with your chosen colour by sifting onto the surface held at right angles to the fall of the grains, over the paper. The layer must cover the copper but should be no thicker, and you should be able to manage without glue. Place the dish on a mesh ready for firing.

3. Fire to 'orange peel' and leave to cool partially before ensuring it can be handled by putting it in water (it could lose shape if doused too quickly). Sand off the loose firescale and stone the edge thoroughly clean. Do not forget that if any firescale can come off, you could easily contaminate your enamel stock.

4. Add a second top coat as before, taking care not to stint the edges, fire and clean.

5. Sprinkle on a third thin coat, place on the mesh and carefully position the

Decorative pieces positioned prior to firing.

Sliding the piece to clean its underside.

mosaics, etc. Make sure that your kiln is really hot, fire until the centre has melted down to the desired level and leave to cool down unaided. (There is now too thick a layer of glass for it to be safe to cool it rapidly in the water.) Clean off the loose firescale.

6. Counter-enamel the cleaned under-side of the piece: sprinkle it with black while holding it at the correct angle, balance it on the palette knife and place it on the three arms of the large stilt. Fire it in this upside down position, just until it is smooth. Repeat if necessary.

7. Stone the edges.

KEEPING PIECES CLEAN

It will become increasingly important that no enamel from the top is left on the back of the piece being lifted, and there are good practices that keep its underneath clean and prevent unwanted grains becoming fired on the wrong side. When putting the knife under the piece in the hand, just prior to finally placing it on the stilt, gently scrape the knife across its underside in case any enamel is sticking to it. Alternatively, and instead of putting

it on the hand, put it on a folded cloth (that old hanky) and push it sideways with the side of the knife against the edge.

VERY SMALL PIECES

Handling any very small pieces can initially present problems: firstly in picking them up and secondly in balancing them on a stilt.

To help pick very small pieces off the working paper, crease the paper down the middle, open this out and place the blank over the indentation from the former

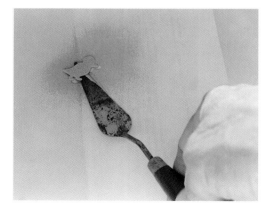

Lifting a small piece.

crease so the knife can be slid up the groove underneath; a pointed palette knife makes this even easier. Another way is to put the piece on top of two spare blanks or coins. Some enamellers find it easier to always have the copper raised above the paper, even when working with bigger sizes of metal.

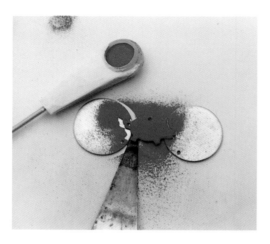

Raising a piece on two bits of copper.

Pieces too small to fit onto any stilt can be fired flat on top of a 'firing pad': a piece of heat-reflective ceramic fibreboard. However, this sometimes marks the enamel on the back of the piece. These pads are needed for the repoussé technique described in Chapter 8 and it might be worth getting one now for more general use.

COLOUR TEST PIECES

You may have noticed that the colour of the grains can differ from how they look when fused. Therefore prepare some example or test pieces for easy reference. (Note that the transparent enamels covered later in this book have their test pieces prepared differently – *see* page 40.)

Mini-Project – Test Pieces for all Opaque Colours

Enamel disks for each of your opaque colours (your blue first piece will do for one). The test pieces can be fixed to the top of the pots with double-sided sticky tape and the exercise will also be good practice for what you have already learnt.

Colour tests on top of enamel pots.

Mini-Project – Enamelled Copper Earrings

For this you will need two identical small blanks. These are enamelled in the usual way but might only require one coat on either side; use the same colour for counter-enamelling. Remember to have the fronts of novelty pieces facing opposite ways so they match when hung from the left and right ears (unless you want two horses chasing themselves in circles round the head!).

Where possible enamel the two side-by-side – on two small twin stilts or a double one – in order to ensure they are identically fired. (It is always useful to have a second small stilt.) After cleaning the edges, thread them on ear-wires.

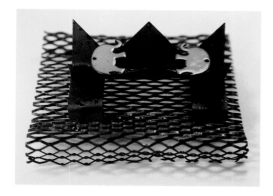

Fired miniature earrings on a double stilt.

Mini-Project – Millefiori Earrings

These are made by slumping down two largish millefiori beads in the kiln and sticking them straight onto a pair of ear-studs. You should do this on a firing pad or a small piece of fireproof tile or mica; therefore, making them may need to be postponed until you have the necessary fireproof surface to support them in the kiln.

Alternatively, they can be fused onto a very small copper base, specially designed for the purpose and which can itself be fired balanced on the side-angle of a twin stilt. Enamel both sides and gum the millefiori bead in place. Dry the gum and fire until it has rounded down, ensure you have no rough places, clean the edges and fit ear-wires.

Fired millefiori on a heat-proof firing pad.

Millefiori earrings with various findings.

Small beads were added to decorate the regular shape of these red loop earrings.

4 Developing the Basics

This chapter introduces further techniques and will help to build up your understanding of the materials and mechanics of enamelling. It will also encourage the development of an individual style.

SOME SIMPLE TOOLS

So far the enamel has been sifted or sprinkled in place, but it can also be manipulated further to achieve the desired effects: just three basic tools are suggested. The first is a small paint brush – an inexpensive size 2 watercolour brush is ideal. The second is made from a large drinking straw and the third uses a sewing needle. These last two are very easily made and have many uses.

A 'quill' can be made from a large plastic drinking straw. The quill is a classical tool for enamelling, but I usually use a prepared straw. This can be readily shaped to suit individual preferences and quickly replaced on wearing out. One end is cut with scissors into a nib shape, more pointed for accuracy, less so for strength. The other end is cut as shown in the photograph below to form a little shovel.

A needle tool can be made from a sewing needle. The point of a needle can

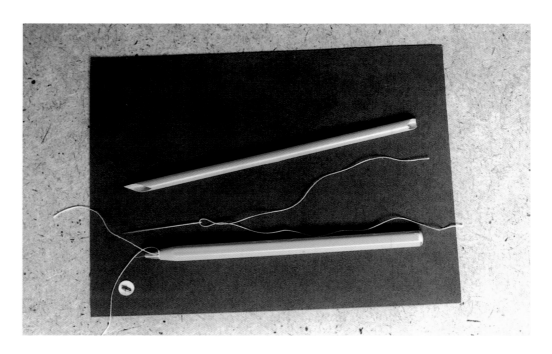

Prepared straw with a needle tool (before its thread is trimmed).

be employed for a number of enamelling functions. A needle with its head stuck into a cork will suffice, but one mounted in a dried-up ballpoint pen case is more comfortable to use.

The inner ink tube and ballpoint are removed with pliers and a medium-sized sewing needle fixed into the space, with ¼in (6mm) of the point sticking out. If the needle is first threaded and positioned with the cotton ends secured on the outside it will not be able to be pushed further back into the case. Plug or glue the needle securely in place.

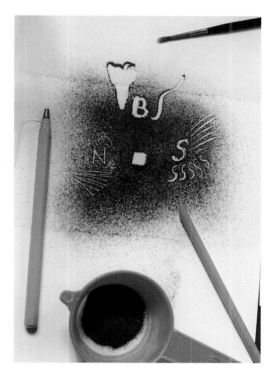

Experiments with tools.

Doodling with Tools

Try the tools out to get familiar with them. Sprinkle some contrasting enamel on a piece of clean shiny paper and prepare two areas, one where the paper is just covered and one with a sparser coat.

Now explore what each of the tools can do, seeing the effect of pushing the grains back to reveal the underlying paper. Continue, but this time try to prevent the enamel piling up by avoiding clearing large areas unless the accumulated grains can be removed entirely from the design. The enamel can be resprinkled as often as you like and eventually returned to its pot.

If you are still experiencing difficulty sprinkling an even coat, try tapping the sieve more gently, or finding one with a smaller mesh through which the grains pass less readily. A specific enamelling '60 mesh' sieve could be the answer to your problems.

Mini-Project – Simple Sgraffito

This is the term for scratching away one layer in order to reveal the underlying one. Try this out on a teddy bear-shaped copper blank. Note that sgraffitoing is easier in fine grains than course ones.

1. Enamel the front dark blue and counter-enamel. (Henceforth I will not always spell out if a second top

Sgraffitoed teddy bear and copper blank.

A Counter-Enamel Pot

It is inevitable that there will be times when it is impossible to keep all the different enamels separate. These cannot be returned to their own pots, so start collecting mixed enamels in a special jar for later use as counter-enamel.

Saddleback pig.

Brushing out the 'saddle'.

coat is required, but take it for granted that the reader will use their judgement, and always counter-enamel a flat piece.)

2 . Cover the top with a normal sprinkling of pale blue and draw in the lines of the joints with the needle tool, taking the displaced grains off the edge of the copper. Add the facial features and, when satisfied, place it carefully on the stilt, fire and finish.

Mini-Project – Using Brush and Straw

In this exercise the brush and straw are used to produce a saddleback pig.

1. Enamel a pig blank white.
2. Cover this with a sprinkling of black, taking care that no white shows through.
3. Brush out the 'saddle' from the pig's back and through the front leg. It is quite likely that a brush stroke will disturb a few grains at the edge of the remaining sprinkled layer: these can be pushed back into place with the side of the straw nib.

4. Mark in the eye and mouth. The needle is probably best for this, and even where you want a wider mark or line it is best to start with a needle mark and then widen it with the point of the straw.
5. Fire and finish.

STENCILS

An alternative way to reveal the white 'saddle' in the last Mini-Project would be to cut a stencil. This makes it easier to place the stripe precisely, but takes longer. Although stencilling works in the obvious manner there are some special points worth considering when sifting on a top colour; once again, have a practice first on paper.

Suppose you have decided that one of the small copper blanks would provide the stencil you want: you will also need to ensure you can lift it off without disturbing the surrounding coat of enamel grains. Fix a small sticky-tape tag on top, covering over any hole in the copper stencil. To lift it off get hold of the tag with tweezers and raise it, taking care not to spill the enamel; this is easier if you are firm, not tentative.

Trial stencil using a copper blank.

Try sprinkling along a straight-edged stencil so you get a sharply defined line from the stencil but a more diffused line on the other side where the grains spread out. To sprinkle in a narrow line use the sifter held at an angle so the powder falls from one side of its mesh, or even get (or make) a small sprinkler only ½in (1cm) or so across. Try again with the stencil held just above the paper and see how the hard line becomes softened. These lines could themselves make an attractive design.

Mini-Project – Using a Paper Stencil

Use a paper or thin card stencil to prepare a two-toned fish. The stencilled area will go right up to the edge of the copper, so cut a stencil that partially covers the copper, but itself goes well beyond it, sideways. The protruding part of the paper can then be handled to remove the stencil.

1. Design and cut the stencil by placing the copper fish blank on the paper, drawing round it and sketching in the line for the stencil (round the body, inside the fins). Mark the position of the fins across this line and cut out, taking the cuts well beyond the fish outline. This will cut the paper in two, giving you two options: a positive and a negative stencil. In this case the body of the fish is to be in the first colour, so will need to be covered by the stencil when sprinkling a second colour for the fins.
2. Enamel the fish in the first (body) colour.
3. Place the stencil over the top side of the body, lining up the marks with the fin positions (the stencil can be held in position by weighing it down

Stencilling a fish.

with a coin or copper blank). Sprinkle on the second colour and remove the stencil.
4. Glue a small bead in place for the eye, but see the suggestion for 'Bead Eyes' if you want to introduce a further refinement.
5. Fire when the glue has dried and finish the piece.

The fish with a beady eye.

FIRESCALE (OXIDIZED COPPER)

The forming of firescale on exposed copper whenever it is fired must be appreciated and controlled. It can be the bane of beginners' lives because the bits of black scale tend to flake off, and because they are so light that they blow about and can contaminate the enamel powder or find their way, as permanent black specks, in

BEAD EYES

Small beads come in useful for eyes on fancy blanks, although they are sometimes inappropriately large. They can be made more 'eye-like' by introducing a black pupil, and I suggest you make a batch at a time.

Select up to a couple of dozen suitable small beads, mix a little black enamel with a drop of glue in the palm of one hand and rub this paste into the beads until the central holes are completely filled, dry and store carefully for future use. Do remember to wash your hands thoroughly.

an otherwise beautifully enamelled surface. These potentially catastrophic results can only be avoided by never letting any partly enamelled piece near your working space until all the loose scale has been removed (from the sides as well as the back); also make sure you clear any scale from around the kiln. It is only later that you will learn how to use this phenomenon in your enamelling.

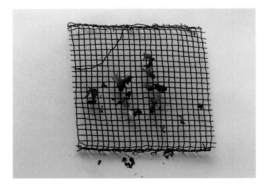

Firescale fallen from the copper back of a fired dish.

Pickling

To date the scale has been removed by hand, but there are times when it is best to clean it off chemically. Instead of using strong acids in the home I prefer the slower, but safer, use of a salt-and-vinegar pickle. Given time a mixture of ordinary vinegar and salt, just about as much salt as the liquid will absorb, will remove the scale from the most stubborn piece. If you want to hasten the process the piece can be taken out, rubbed with a soft saucepan cleaner to clear anything already loosened and put back into the pickle to remove more.

If the smell offends you, keep the pickle in a covered plastic container; do not keep it once it goes green (from the copper) and avoid putting your fingers into the pot, as it makes fingernails difficult to clean.

MORE ABOUT FIRING ENAMELS

Each enamel has its own characteristics, quite apart from its colouring, and a new enameller will soon notice slight differences in how they fire. I am deliberately not naming most of the ones I use, as the choice is vast and it is important that you get to know those you possess.

Start a notebook and record the number, manufacturer and supplier of each enamel. Begin by adding your observations on whether you like it, if it seems to fire slowly or quickly and anything else of note.

There are a few general points that you may have already noticed:

- Many enamels temporarily take on quite a different colour while hot; for example, yellow looks red.
- Most reds and many yellows and oranges have a tendency to burn out rather readily, turning dark at the edges and sometimes even disappearing where the enamel is put on thinly; that means that special care is needed in ensuring that the edges are always well covered; these enamels also usually require more (not thicker) coats.
- Burn-out is increasingly likely when the kiln is at its hottest or the piece left in it for too long, becoming 'over-fired'.
- Some opaque enamels such as mazarine blue develop a translucence when fired at a high temperature.

All these variations are partly due to which oxide has been used to provide the colouring, and expensive oxides also account for higher prices, such as when gold is used for reds.

THE MELTING TEMPERATURE

Most enamels are designed to melt at temperatures a little under 800°C but differences in this temperature mean that some enamels seem to melt more quickly than others; this is often an introduced characteristic. Those melting at the lowest temperature are said to be 'soft' while 'hard' enamels require higher than average temperatures.

SOFT UNDER HARD ENAMELS

Spectacular results can be achieved by firing a hard enamel on top of a coat of a differently coloured soft enamel. The undercoat will melt again ('remelt') first and 'bubble through' the top colour in the kiln. Test pieces and good records of the results are essential to successfully capitalize on this phenomenon. There can be enamelled on scraps of copper but I find that they are more likely to be kept and enjoyed when incorporated into something potentially attractive.

PROJECT – TEST DISH: SIX COLOURED OPAQUE ENAMELS OVER SOFT WHITE

Six differently coloured enamels will be tried out on a shallow 3in (8cm) dish using a stencil to separate them. They can

be put on in 60-degree segments or, as in this example, a more interesting design. The choice is yours, but you must give bold patches of separate colours.

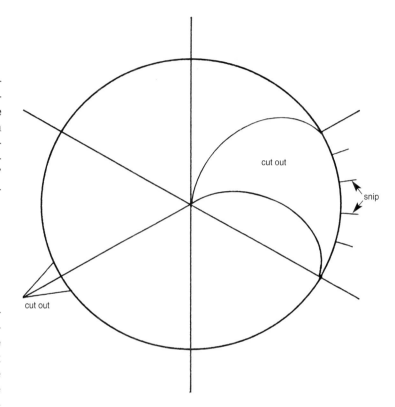

A stencil for a segmented dish.

1. Make your design by first drawing round the outline of the dish and dividing it into six. Adapt one segment to accurately plan the stencil for a single colour, then cut it out of thin card, leaving an outer frame at least 1in (2.5cm) beyond the circle. Add a snipped 'V' opposite, but outside the circle, to help position the stencil. The stencil will be used in turn for each of six enamels, so try it out first with any enamel on the copper dish.
2. Fit the stencil, with the outer arc of the cut-out segment just tucked behind the rim of the dish (a few small snips across the circumference line may help), and hold the card

Practising sprinkling a segment of the dish.

gets to the orange peel stage. Clean off the firescale.

4. Decide on the positioning of the colours; they are all going to be stencilled before being fired together so it is essential that every precaution is taken to prevent any cross-contamination. It could also help, in positioning the stencil, if you put a small temporary tag of sticky tape on the dividing line between the segments, but out of the way, underneath the edge of the dish, leaving just a bit showing.

5. Stencil the first colour as practised. (Take your time!)

6. Carefully put the dish down, lift off the stencil and clean off the excess enamel from both sides. On this first application any stray grains on the dish could be removed but there will inevitably be a little overlap at the edges between the colours.

7. Having removed all traces of the first colour from your working area, go ahead with stencilling the next. Repeat with all the remaining enamels, trying to align them evenly. Use the tags as guidelines, but gently peel them off before firing.

across the dish with your thumb so it rests lightly on the rest of the rim as you nestle the dish in your left hand. Sprinkle into the segment with the grains falling vertically onto the copper by angling the dish slightly. Put on an even, but slightly sparse coat (the copper should still just show through). When you are happy with the trial save the enamel and clean the dish.

3. Put a normal coat of soft white enamel on the inside. Fire it but be alert to the soft enamel firing quickly and try to remove it from the kiln as soon as it

Six-coloured dish, sprinkled and ready to fire.

8. Fire in a hot kiln until bubbling can be seen in some sectors. Do not be afraid to put the dish back in the kiln if you think it needs longer, but try not to let any of the enamels burn out.

9. Cool the dish and clean off the loose firescale. Pickling is the ideal way to clean off the firescale, but there is another catch in this particular case: it is better not to immerse any soft enamel in even as mild an acid as vinegar. (This does not apply to other enamels.)

   Consequently, pickle the dish by placing it flat in a container and pouring in the pickle so it just rises to the rim but does not get into the dish and into contact with the soft white enamel. Clean and polish.

10. Note your results. For example, in the test shown below: 'dark blue – bold spots', 'red and orange – small spots particularly where thinnest', 'yellow – spots, but hardly showing', 'pale blue – poor spotting' and 'green – nothing'. You can safely assume that this green (fir) is as soft as the white.

    Note that you could now counter-enamel the back, observing the results of this second firing on the front –

some sectors would be likely to have improved but the red would probably have burnt out significantly. However, a small enamelled dish that is to be reasonably carefully handled has enough intrinsic strength (because of its shape) for counter-enamelling to be unnecessary.

11. Varnish. Applying several coats of metal varnish onto the polished copper is an accepted way to finish your enamel.

FURTHER SUPPLIES

When topping up your supplies, get ready to progress to the next chapter by considering buying some transparent enamels, twenty or so small rectangles about ⅜ × 1in (1 × 3cm) for tests and some larger flat pieces copper, about 3in × 2in (5cm × 7.5cm) for small pictures. Also a few larger circular pieces or ovals, 2in (5cm) or larger, for pendants or brooches will come in handy before long.

MORE ABOUT THE COMPOSITION OF ENAMELS

In the UK the majority of enamellers use the lead-bearing enamels (supplied with most kits), but lead-free enamels are easily available. However, the two types are not always compatible, so it might be wiser to keep to one or the other.

Enamels are sold in lump or powder form. A pestle and mortar is needed to crush the lump to a powder, which should be done with the lumps under water to prevent the bits flying about. The prepared powdered enamels, as used for sprinkling, are ground into small grains that will pass through a mesh with sixty holes per square inch, and the consis-

Dish with a polished and varnished copper underside.

TIPS

- You can keep stencils for further use.
- In a small kiln, you can reverse a larger piece if the part near the door is slow to fire.

The fired spotted dish.

tency in their sizing affects the quality of the enamelling. Some enamels are supplied more evenly graded than others but, although problems seldom occur when dusting on an even coat, they become very apparent if the grains get really wet, unless all the finest dusty particles have been removed. One solution is to wash them out.

Lump enamel being crushed.

WASHING ENAMELS

Working with wet enamels facilitates many more advanced techniques, but it is essential for them to be washed first. Ideally, the first stage is to freshen the grains in a small mortar, giving them a brief regrind with the pestle. However, you can leave out this stage until you have acquired a small pestle and mortar for enamelling (the same type as used for cooking but not the same set!).

The Washing Procedure

1. Put a little enamel in the mortar, cover with water and give the grains a short regrinding by rocking the pestle, rather than stirring.

2. Wash the enamel either in the mortar, a small bowl or an artist's ceramic pallet. Alternatively, you could use plastic single-helping jam containers, or even cut yoghurt pots down to the bottom ¼in (1cm).

Washing enamels in a plastic tray.

3. When covered with water the larger grains will sink while the smallest remain suspended briefly, making the water look cloudy. During washing, tap the side of the container to encourage the larger grains to settle. Pour off the 'milky' water once the larger grains have separated, taking care to remove the dusty particles only, not the clean grains. Repeat this procedure until the water remains clear.

    Give the enamel two final washes, preferably with water from a domestic purifier or, even better, distilled water. This eliminates any chemical impurities in the tap water.

4. Cover the washed grains but use them on the same day. If kept they must be dried; they are then highly suitable for sifting. Note the enamel's identification in pencil on the container.

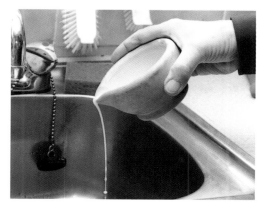

Pouring off the fine grains in the 'milky' first wash.

WET LAYING

Sprinkled enamel grains are not as easily positioned as those applied when wet. But under water, the smallest grains soon rise to the top and will probably leave a mark when fired; so these must have been got rid of beforehand. There is an art in laying the wet grains and it requires some practice. If you have the grains too wet they will slide about uncontrollably, but if too dry they will not lie flat.

Wet enamel being picked up from the edge of the water.

Prop the dish of washed enamel up at a slight angle, with some of the grains under water and some above it. Use a straw (quill), small paintbrush or whatever suits you to pick up some grains from the edge of the water, where it is neither too wet nor too dry. Place the grains in as even a layer as possible, if necessary controlling the dampness by adding more water with the brush or drawing some off by touching the edge with a cloth or tissue.

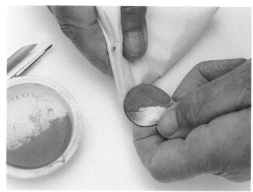

Moisture being sucked off into a tissue.

Mini-Project – Wet-Lay an Oval

1. Use a small oval, preferably domed, counter-enamel it and clean the top by pickling (*see* page 30) before giving it a final rub with the abrasive sponge.
2. Wash some cream enamel (or any pale colour).
3. Wet-lay the top – this is sometimes easiest to do holding the piece in your left hand or on your finger tips. You may even find it better to place your piece down and pull enamel from the straw with the needle tool or brush; either tool can also be used to spread the wet grains.

TIPS

- Large lumps can be split, wrapped in strong cloth and hit with a hammer.
- Plastic spoons are handy for handling very small quantities of washed enamel.
- Avoid making your wet laying too deep, otherwise enamel may flake off.

Wet-laid piece being tapped to make it level off.

While it is still quite wet, tap the edge with the knife or a pencil and the layer should level out; then draw off the excess water with a tissue.

4. As soon as you have satisfactorily wet-laid the piece, dry it thoroughly (possibly on top of the kiln) and fire.

5. One coat may be enough to give a good finish on a small piece; if not, just give it another. Use it for the next mini-project.

Mini-Project – Oriental Tree Brooch

1. Design a simple pseudo-Chinese tree to fit this oval, with a chunky, angular stem and hanging flowers.

2. Wash a little brown enamel and possibly some yellow or blue for the flowers, though you may prefer to stick on small chippings for these.

3. Wet-lay the brown. The enamel should stay in place, but covering the oval with a thin layer of gum first will help further. (It does not matter if gum dries out, as the water from the enamel will re-activate its adhesiveness.)

4. Add the flowers, dry and fire, taking the piece out of the kiln while the pattern is still in relief. Finish and attach a brooch pin.

Wet laying is particularly useful when you want the enamel to look slightly proud or undulating on the last firing: take it only fractionally past the 'orange peel' stage. An example of this is shown in the photograph below where it has been used to emphasise the bobbles of a poodle's trim.

Poodle showing its 'bobbles' in relief.

Wet laying is equally ideal on minute pieces or when laying two colours side-by-side. The photograph below shows how it could be used to lay blue and red on bird earrings, for swallows.

Wet laid tree design with chips (flowers) being glued in place.

Swallow earrings wet-laid in blue and red.

STONING ENAMELS

Fired enamel can be stoned back with a carborundum stone. A coarse one easily removes stilt marks from the back of a piece, but a less harsh one is best for obtaining a really flat finish on a piece already enamelled with two or three top coats. The action of stoning creates a potentially contaminating fine dust from both the stone and the enamel, so it should be done under running water and the piece given a final scrub with a bristle or, better still, a glass brush. (You could keep a strong nail brush just for enamelling.) The resulting roughened surface must be 'flash fired' before it has had time to pick up any impurities: that is, given a quick refiring to restore its glossy finish.

This method is excellent when a perfectly flat, smooth surface is essential, as when preparing to use painting enamels

(*see* page 62): the whole surface of the pre-enamelled blank is stoned back until it all looks matt. If it is not reasonably flat in the first place it needs a preliminary stoning, then wet-laying more enamel in any shiny looking depressions, drying, refiring and a repeat stoning until it is really level and can be given its final flash firing.

TRANSFERS

Competent artists will want to use the specially prepared, finely ground painting enamels, but the less experienced may enjoy trying commercially prepared transfers, which are supplied in many beginner's kits. They are often designed to fit specific shapes of copper blank.

Transfers are prepared with painting enamels printed on the underside of a sheet of protective lacquer that will burn off on firing. This is mounted on a bit of paper that separates when soaked in tepid water.

Mini-Project – an Enamelled Transfer

1. Using a butterfly shape and matching transfer, enamel the copper with hard or normal white, getting it really flat as described under 'Stoning Enamels'.
2. Soak the transfer in tepid water. When the picture (right side up) floats clear of the paper, slip the prepared blank under it and position it carefully with a paint brush. Gentle pressure with a tissue, applied from the centre outwards, will remove much of the water and any trapped air bubbles, but the piece should be left an hour or two in a warm place to dry completely.

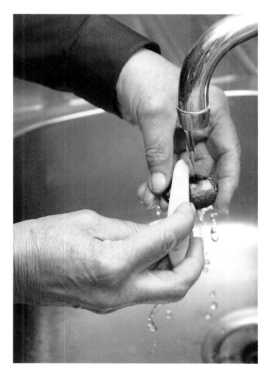

Stoning the surface flat.

Floating transfer being positioned onto a prepared blank.

3. Fire in a normally heated kiln but leave the door slightly open initially, to let out the fumes as the flammable coat burns off. This soon happens, usually with some smoke and possibly a brief flame. The door is then shut (on a now only moderately hot kiln) so the design can fire onto the base. Be careful not to overfire it, by removing the butterfly as soon as it goes shiny.

4. Finish and attach a brooch pin.

Enamelled transfer butterfly brooch.

5 Introducing Transparent Enamels

INTRODUCTION

Once you have mastered the basics covered in the previous two chapters you will be on your way to becoming a proficient enameller, albeit still at a basic level. The introduction of transparents will add a new dimension.

Artists sometimes argue that watercolour painting is more difficult than using oils because those working in the watercolours always have to consider what shows through the top colour, while those using oil or acrylic paints can cover up their mistakes! There is some similarity for the enameller.

Transparent enamels are worked in exactly the same way as opaques, even though their appearance and effect differ. The opaques' lack of clarity is caused by the introduction of an opacifier during its manufacture and, without this, every mark on the underlying copper is liable to remain visible. Therefore it must be scrupulously clean and, in particular, free from firescale.

Fluxes

When using transparent enamels a clear, colourless enamel, called a flux, is usually put directly over the copper to enhance any subsequent colours; it also

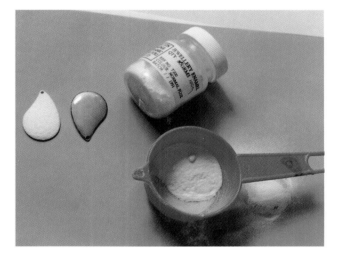

One coat of flux, both unfired and fired.

glazes the metal. There are many varieties but 'normal' or 'copper' flux will be used in most instances. Fluxes can also be hard or soft (alternatively 'diamond' or 'silver'), with the soft one behaving similarly to a soft white. Therefore it is ideal for special effects similar to those tried out in the last chapter and is well worth possessing. Note that powdered fluxes look white before they are fired.

Mini-Project – Fluxing Copper

1. Sprinkle a normal, but not too thick, layer of flux onto a clean, copper base, and fire it. It may initially

appear slightly red, when just fused; this is immaterial as its true colour-lessness will be restored with further firing. What is important is that it should be clear, without any of the cloudiness probably caused by underfiring, applying it too thickly or using an enamel with an irregular grain size. All transparent colours can look cloudy for similar reasons.

2. Counter-enamel, clean the edges, fire on another coat of flux and keep it for later use.

TRANSPARENT COLOURS

The appearance of a transparent enamel will alter when fired over different underlying layers. There are three bases that specially interest us now: the copper itself, flux and white enamel.

As with the opaque enamels, each transparent colour must have an example enamelled for reference, but this time the enamel is put over the three bases on the same bit of copper. These can take the form of a disk with three segments, stuck on the top of each pot, but I prefer to keep my 'pallet of transparents' separately, with similar colours grouped together. Originally I stapled them into a plastic sleeve, but now I use a little photograph album, as in the photograph below.

A page of transparent colour test pieces.

Mini-Project – Preparing Test Pieces

1. Counter-enamel at least one of the small rectangular bars for each of your transparent colours, pickle and sprinkle flux on one end, using a stencil.

The stages in preparing test strips for colour tests.

2. Fire, pickle and stencil white on the other end. Fire and pickle again, and you are ready to use the bars to test the effects of each transparent enamel.

3. Rub the bare copper section in the centre really clean, sprinkle the whole bar with a colour and fire. You will now see how it looks on flux, copper or white. A second layer, stencilled lengthways over half the bar can show how each looks under two layers of colour.

Prepared transparent colour tests.

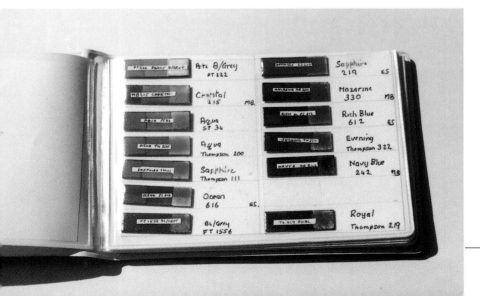

4. Repeat for all the colours but do make sure not to loose track of which bar refers to which enamel! Label each bar and mount in whatever way you choose.

Mini-Project – Overlaying the Flux

1. Look at your test colours, select one you like when seen over flux and use it to cover the blank you originally fluxed. (Normally one coat of flux suffices as a base for transparent enamel.)
2. Fire one coat, note its appearance and fire on a second coat. Make a note of any deepening of the hue, and of any other observed characteristics.
3. Add a millefiori bead or other pieces of decorative media, selecting opaque or transparent bits in a blending colour.

Transparents can be used very successfully for many of the examples given in Chapters 3 and 4. By now you should be getting plenty of your own ideas: try them out and remember to keep notes.

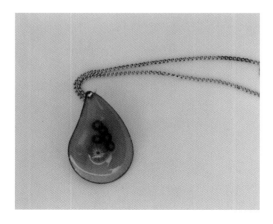

Transparent millefiori on gold-coloured enamel.

EXPERIMENTS

Consider using transparents for stencilling, bearing in mind their density as well as their hue – a light or pastel colour will hardly show over a dense one. Think about the effect of superimposing a transparent enamel that still reveals, and therefore changes, the colour underneath. As in watercolour painting it could be risky superimposing two very different transparent colours (for example, green over red could just cancel the beauty of each colour), but intermediate shades may be possible. If in doubt always enamel a test piece to see the effect, and do experiment: the oak leaf shown below was one beginner's first trial piece, stencilling a strong green over a pastel transparent background colour. Would the addition of a red or brown acorn work? And where?

A beginner's trial with transparents.

Your Finished Pieces

You will now be well aware of various choices of how to finish and present a piece, so only the occasional suggestions will be given. Also, expect to have occasional enamelling failures, but keep them for reference and possibly reuse later.

Mini-Project – Testing Over a Soft Enamel

Most transparents are hard (high-firing) enough to produce the bubbly effect over soft white, so try some of the stronger colours out. (The effect will be hardly noticeable in pale transparents.) Try this out with several different enamels on any copper shape. The effects will be similar when firing over a soft flux, but the 'bubbles' will be the colour of fluxed copper – so try this too – using a colour that looked good over the fluxed end of the test piece.

PROJECT – A PENDANT USING SGRAFFITO IN SOFT WHITE

The design depends on a few sgraffitoed lines that will appear dark if the firescale is left where it forms; on the effect of soft white bubbling through a hard transparent colour; and finally on the tendency of a soft enamel base to move downwards when molten and fired in a sloping position.

1. Choose one of the larger domed pendant shapes and a suitable colour, then plan simple sgraffito marks, according to its shape.

Working drawing for decorative sgraffito lines.

2. Counter-enamel first and pickle the front.
3. Sprinkle the soft white over a damp coat of gum on the front, leave to dry, sgraffito the lines and tip off the loosened white grains, then fire the piece.
4. Sprinkle on the transparent and fire it flat on a stilt, just until it fuses.

Pendant using the effects obtainable from enamels with different melting temperatures.

The piece supported for firing at an angle.

5. Prop up the pendant at an angle using a bent piece of wire from the edge of a mesh and re-fire it in a hot kiln until the design starts to slip downwards, but take it out of the kiln as soon as enamel begins to build up at the bottom, and certainly before it runs off the piece. This requires close observation, as the timing is critical.

6. If some of the glass fuses to the mesh, carefully pull the cooled piece free and stone it down or add some more enamel to make it good, before giving it a quick refire flat on a stilt. Anyone with a bigger firing chamber could sandwich a firing pad between two meshes for stage 5 so as to be absolutely sure that no enamel runs onto the kiln floor.

Hand-shaped dish combining the effects of soft white and harder transparent enamels. Can you see how it was enamelled using opaques as well as transparents over the soft white?

CARE OF THE KILN

Should enamel accidentally get on the floor or side of the kiln it should be treated with kaolin (from a chemist), 'bat wash' or 'kiln wash'. These are china clay-based substances that can be brushed onto the enamel patch as a paste, when the kiln is cold, and that will absorb the molten enamel when the chamber is heated. However, do not do this more often than absolutely necessary. Never leave a kiln on full power when not in use.

CARE OF STILTS AND MESHES

Enamel should be kept off these supports as far as possible, but inevitably some will occasionally fuse to them. Remove lumps forming on a mesh by pinching the wire with small-nosed pliers while holding it in a cloth to prevent bits flying about. The edges of stilts (where the enamelled piece is balanced) and the top of a mesh can be cleaned back to the steel with an ordinary file.

Avoid immersing hot stainless steel stilts or meshes in water, as it accelerates their deterioration. Nevertheless, they may eventually need to be discarded – immediately if any bits start to flake off.

PROJECT – GOLD-BEARING TRANSFERS

Some of the most attractive commercial transfers contain gold, and these can look particularly striking when fused onto a transparent base coat.

1. Select a colour or colours that will complement those of the transfer, often just gold and black, and prepare the blank with at least two coats of the transparent enamel.

2. Proceed as with the Mini-Project on page 37, remembering to dry the piece

A Soft White 'Mesh' Design

Try manipulating a very thin dusting of soft white with the straw and brush to create an open netting-like pattern. Sprinkle it over a colourful blank and the soft white will be softer-looking than a normal white.

Gold and black transfer.

for several hours, or overnight, and being very careful not to overfire it.

MORE ABOUT THE COPPER

Standard small copper blanks are usually about 1mm thick (20 or 22 gauge). However, bigger pieces are often enamelled on something slightly thicker, while a much thinner sheet is used for other techniques, especially repoussé, where the copper is raised by hand.

Annealing

Copper becomes harder when stressed by working, but can be made considerably more flexible again by annealing; that is, by heating it until it is nearly red hot and cooling again – plunging it into cold water will remove much of the newly formed firescale. Annealing also burns out all the impurities, can be repeated as often as necessary, and occurs naturally while enamelling a piece.

The copper in a newly enamelled piece is surprisingly soft and, after firing with just one coat, can have slight distortions pushed out by hand on a flat surface. This may weaken the enamel, but its strength will be restored with the next firing.

A flat piece that has lost shape during the application of several coats can also be flattened. Take the enamel from the kiln and while it is still partially molten, press it down with an old flat iron on a piece of steel plate: possibly the top of the kiln. It is advisable to have both the iron and the steel plate partially preheated, and of course absolutely clean. This procedure requires every caution and a lot of courage, but it works.

Flattening a hot enamel plate.

CUTTING YOUR OWN COPPER SHAPES

It is often more rewarding to create your own shapes, and much of this can be done with a pair of tin snips and other household tools. Look out for 'aviation shears' – they are double-levered, and so easy to work and probably cheaper. However, use a piercing saw if you have one.

Adapting Pre-Shaped Blanks

Changing the shape of an annealed copper blank is easy. A regular shape can be slightly domed by hand simply by pressing its edge at an angle on a rigid flat surface, and going round the shape once or twice. Similarly, some distortion in a dish can be removed by turning the bowl over and pushing it down to level its rim on a flat tile.

Standard copper shapes can be adapted. A horse-shaped blank could have its rein removed or its head filed down to a zebra's profile.

Horse blank and adaptations.

3. Use pliers, preferably round-nosed, to turn back the loop and file the edges flat if necessary.
4. If you like, re-anneal and dome it.

COMBINING COPPER PIECES

You can make a large picture by combining smaller pieces that individually fit easily into the kiln. A montage of regular commercial blanks can be pleasing, and those who are prepared to saw out their own pieces could be more ambitious.

A picture composed of many regularly shaped pieces, designed by Kathleen Kay and enamelled by her special needs students at Dudley College.

Mini-Project – Cutting a Pendant with a Loop Top

1. Design a pendant shape with a tab, that can be turned behind to form a loop, and copy it on thin paper or greaseproof paper.
2. Paste this onto some annealed copper sheet with ordinary paper glue, cut out the shape (following the outline) and soak off the paper.

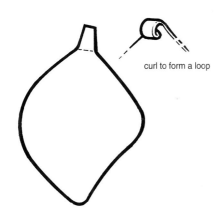

curl to form a loop

A hand-cut pendant design.

'The Clown' (cut into pieces, enamelled and reassembled) by Ann Jewell.

A MIST SPRAY

A fine mist spray, filled with distilled water, is often useful when applying the enamel. It will become an essential aid to more advanced enamelling techniques and will be needed for the next project, so it is well worth acquiring one now. Old scent sprays, professional hair sprays (empty ones are easily begged from most hairdressers) or even garden sprays will do, provided they are cleaned first and have as fine a spray as possible.

PROJECT – THE STANDING TORTOISE

This animal is made from flat copper sheet with pliers and a hammer, plus a largish flat-ended screwdriver and a big nail, both used as punches. It was formed on some old carpeting on the floor, that offered a soft but reasonably rigid surface on which to hammer and shape the copper.

The standing tortoise.

Design for the 3D tortoise.

1. Stick a tracing of the shape onto some annealed copper as a temporary guide and cut it out.

Punching the shell pattern.

2. Pencil in and punch the shell's pattern on the underside in a series of rough pentagons by hammering the screwdriver down. It is then turned over for the toes to be marked on the feet; use the point of the nail for the eyes and to indent each pentagon centrally.
3. Soften the copper again by re-annealing. Re-punch the shell pattern, doming the body as you work by angling the copper on the carpet. The head, legs and tail are rounded with pliers, and the feet and (optional) tail pushed downwards and adjusted so the tortoise stands on all four feet and the overall shape looks right.
4. Pickle it to remove the firescale.
5. Select an enamel that looks good directly over copper and whose transparency will allow the indentations to appear dark, contrasting with the raised parts.
6. The enamel is sprinkled on top, over a thin layer of gum, while the copper

shape is positioned to ensure an even covering. In order to get enough enamel adhering to this three-dimensional piece, sprinkle on a thin coat, spray it lightly all over with distilled water (again turning it to ensure an even distribution) and add another thin sprinkling of enamel. Hold the spray well away from the object so only the finest droplets reach the enamel.

The water dampening the first coat will take up the gum and allow the second coat to stick to it, so the piece can be well covered with a normal thickness of enamel. Be careful not to overdo the spraying – if it gets really wet the enamel could slip or the fine grains rise to cause a loss of clarity.

7. Dry, fire and pickle. Then enamel the underside in the same way – the gum will hold the grains in position while it is fired, on a mesh, standing on its feet.
8. The top will almost certainly need another application of the enamel.

MORE STILT SHAPES

Ingenuity is often the answer to how to support enamels in the kiln, but fashioning one-off shapes from old tin cans is not recommended because of the risk of cutting oneself. However, a W-shaped mesh can be bent to suit many awkward shapes and most small dishes.

These can be bent out of a strip, approximately 3½in (9cm) wide, cut from one of the available 1ft (30cm) squares of mesh. Its useful height will depend on the size of your kiln chamber, and the bends can be positioned to allow lifting either with the firing fork or, in the case of a small kiln, a broad kitchen-sized palette knife. The top can be bent and adapted to minimize or eliminate contact with the enamel, and consequential stilt marks.

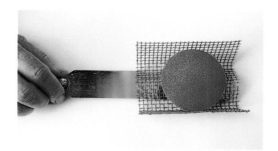
Small W-shaped mesh being lifted with a broad pallet knife.

OPAQUE AND TRANSPARENT ENAMELS COMBINED

Transparent enamels behind areas of opaque colours create a very useful illusion of depth.

PROJECT – STENCILLED LEAF DISH

Use a leaf as a pattern for a stencil and to give the overall outline of the dish. The maximum size will depend on what fits into your kiln, but designs are easily adapted using the reduction facilities of a photocopier.

1. Select a leaf with an interesting outline – the one illustrated overleaf comes from a lemon-scented geranium.
2. Draw round its outline. To arrive at the eventual shape of the dish, put a further line outside this, following the leaf's general shape but leaving out the indentations. Outside this draw another line ½in (1cm) away.

Hand-formed leaf dish and the stencil removed in stage 10.

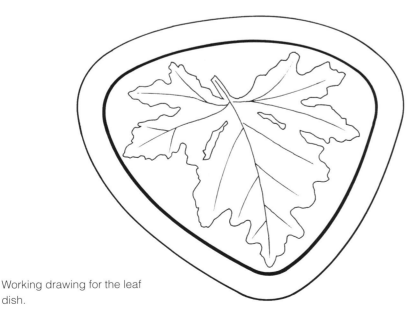

Drawing round the leaf.

Working drawing for the leaf dish.

3. Cut this larger shape from softened copper plate, anneal again and mark the extent of the flat bottom of the dish by temporarily sticking on a tracing the size of the smaller dish shape.
4. Bend up the sides by holding them at an angle against some wood and gently hammering into the part where the bend is required, using the round end of a hammer. Refine the shape with pliers, annealing again whenever necessary.

Bending up the sides of the dish.

5. Counter-enamel the underside of the dish once with black enamel.
6. Adapt a W-shaped mesh to hold the dish securely while enamelling the inside.
7. Enamel the centre of the dish with flux and two or three coats of transparent red, each time pickling off any firescale on the exposed copper perimeter.
8. Cut a stencil of the exact shape of the leaf. As this is probably bigger and more complicated than any used before a new method is recommended: cut it from blotting paper or, better still, the more durable absorbent paper from a coffee filter.

9. Choose a darkish-green opaque enamel, cover the inside of the dish with gum, place the (slightly dampened) stencil accurately and sprinkle on the green: angle the dish as you work and spray to keep the stencil and enamel damp (not wet) as you build up a normal layer of enamel.

10. While it is still damp, carefully remove the stencil with tweezers. The outline should be crisp and the enamel on top of the moist paper should not fall off. (The stencil can be dried, cleaned and kept, and the enamel saved.)

The dish after its final firing, reversed on its mesh.

Lifting off the absorbent stencil while still damp.

11. Fire when dry and, if necessary, the stencil can be replaced and a second coat of green added.

12. If there are unsightly stilt marks these can be stoned flat, possibly touched up, and the dish given a second coat of counter-enamel, upside down in such a position that no enamel touches the 'W' mesh.

DRY ENAMELLED PICTURES

The scope for enamelling pictures is vast. Many use specialized enamelling paints and some are wet-laid with washed enamels, but an impressionistic style can also be achieved by sprinkling and manipulating dry enamels. Even those who have no pretensions to being able to paint should at least have a try. The result may not be exactly what was intended, but if you have a flexible approach you may be very pleased with the outcome. The seaside scene overleaf was one beginner's very early effort.

Get your ideas from pictures, cards or photographs and be prepared to simplify them. Decide on the overall background tone: is it to be transparent or opaque, and would a first covering of flux or white, or even some of each, give you a useful starting point as your first coat of enamel?

Secondly, on a piece of paper, sketch out vaguely where you want the general blocks of colour, such as blue sky, mid-green trees, light green grass and grey building. Decide whether a transparent enamel would look best. Also, do you want to leave gaps for clouds in the sky? Would the buildings or a prominent tree

'Seaside View' by Maureen Astle.

be better left until they can be superimposed more accurately once the second coat is fired in place?

Also bear in mind the following general points:

◆ You can add the main features on top, in as many firings as you want.

◆ Most red, and some orange, enamels burn out easily, and so are best applied last.

◆ At all stages the enamel can be sprinkled with an ordinary or small sieve, overlapped, shielded from areas with stencils, manipulated with any of the tools or brushed off altogether.

◆ As your confidence increases you could even incorporate the bubble-through effects of softer enamels and the burn-out of thin layers. Touching up with painting enamel will become another option.

The next project illustrates the method. Try either this picture, or a simple picture of your own choice.

PROJECT – A SMALL PICTURE, 'THE RUINED CASTLE'

1. Prepare a 2 × 3in (5 × 7½cm) rectangular piece of copper with two layers of counter-enamel, pressing as flat as you can by hand and pickling after each firing. The picture size can be increased according to the size of kiln. Round off the corners of rectangular pictures slightly, with a file.

2. For this picture the background is sprinkled all over with an even coat of normal white, and a natural look is enhanced by not making it too dense. A little soft white was also added through a slit in a stencil to create an interesting central hedge, but this can be left out.

3. The main blocks of intermediate colouring are added by sprinkling transparents quite thinly and using a stencilled skyline cut out of a piece of thin card about twice the size of the picture. The bottom half is positioned to sprinkle the blue sky. The top stencil is then supported just above this while the hills, central wood and foreground are added, in various greens and olive, right across the

'The Ruined Castle' – a dry-sifted enamelled picture.

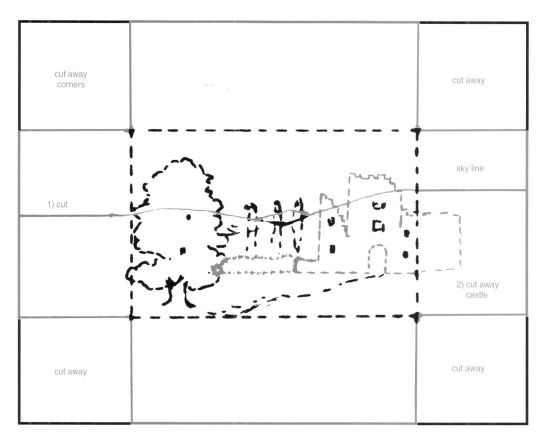

Working sketch for
colouring stencils.

cut away
corners

cut away

sky line

1) cut

2) cut away
castle

cut away

cut away

Stencils (Red lines)

1) Skyline stencil ─────
2) Castle stencil ------------
3) Hedge stencil +++++++
   (optional)

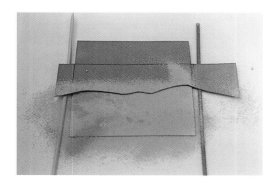

Stencilling the background greens, with the sky
shielded.

plate. Firing the plate fixes these background colours, leaving the castle, some central trees and the big tree to be to be superimposed afterwards.

4. Make and use a stencil for the ruined castle, sprinkling in an opaque stone colour and refining its shape with the straw tool. On the left-hand side sprinkle a little black and then some opaque dark green on top of this, and shape the big tree by brushing off some enamel from the beyond the outline. If you have not got a small enough sieve to ensure none of the tree sprinkling falls over the stonework, you can shield it with paper. Most of the central trees can be left for the next firing, but if you can introduce some of them without disturbing the castle and the big tree they can be placed at this stage. Fire.

5. The remaining central trees are added by putting on more opaque greens,

Flux and Transparent Backgrounds

The sunflowers in this picture were enamelled on a flux and transparent coloured background. Opaques can be added afterwards.

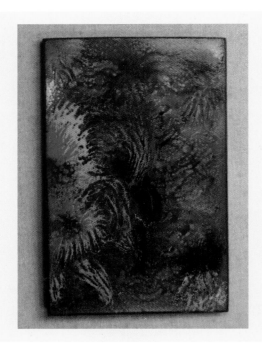

with either end of the straw and pushing the grains into place. Add the tree trunk in the same way and break up the evenness of the foreground with a few patches of transparent olives or fawns.

6. It is probably safest to fire these in place before finishing the picture by accentuating the contours of the tree with some paler green opaque enamel, using black for the castle archway and windows, and indicating shading on the castle and tree trunk. An extra firing also makes it possible to 'tittivate' the picture and introduce the sheep in the foreground using some soft white.

Be prepared to adapt your original design as you go. Hopefully it will satisfy you, but it can always be adjusted by stoning back or adding more enamel and refiring.

6 More Advanced Artistic Techniques

Yolu should now be gaining confidence in many basic ways of using enamels and be selecting the techniques you prefer to achieve the desired effects. I now want to introduce a few new ideas that can stand on their own, or be incorporated in more complex pieces of enamelling, thereby adding to your artistic options. In this chapter we will look at swirling and the use of silver foil and of supersoft flux, and there will be an introduction to enamel painting.

NEW SUPPLIES REQUIRED

Swirling, also incorporating scrolling, involves manipulating the molten enamel with that long, turned-down, pointed tool, the 'swirling tool', included in most kits. It primarily uses the enamels you already have, including lumps or chips. However, many newcomers to this method so enjoy it that they soon need more mixed colours of transparent lump.

Look ahead to see if you would like any of the illustrated copper shapes, and you will also need to buy at least a single 6in (150mm) square of silver foil to explore its use. Some 'supersoft flux' will be required for the third new technique and, although it appears relatively expensive, a little goes a long way.

Painting with enamels is an art in its own right and as such is not covered in this book, but I am including enough information for enamel paints to be used to give a more professional finish to pieces enamelled in other techniques. Those who only want to try them, or use them to add to their general enamelling, do not need to buy a full set of colours but could start with five pre-mixed tubes: black, white and the primary colours red, blue and yellow. Alternatively, get a sample set of overglaze painting enamels (normally twelve phials), including the same basic five. These are very finely ground and are usually mixed with an oil 'painting medium': there are proprietary brands available but lavender oil, turpentine or glycercol will do and you can even try pure water. Enamels are painted with small brushes ranging in size from '000' to '2', and you will need at least one of these.

SWIRLING

The decorations to be swirled must be placed on a piece prepared with at least two top coats of enamel. These must be heated until they liquify sufficiently for the tool to be pulled across the surface, moving the enamel with ease, without being pressed down to the metal. To achieve this a small kiln will probably be

A swirled brooch.

almost at its maximum temperature (approaching 900°C) and the piece may well need to be left in for longer than usual, until the enamel flattens into a molten pool. The tip of the tool should also be briefly pre-heated against the hot side of the chamber, or in a gas flame.

Swirling is done in an open kiln, but while losing as little heat as possible. Therefore the movement of the tool should be pre-planned, not too elaborate and executed quite quickly. Once done, the kiln door is shut again for a brief further firing, that lets the tool mark heal and the piece level off. The tool will probably raise some molten enamel when it is lifted off the piece, giving a visible tail to the swirl and leaving some sticking to the point of the tool; dip it into water to clear off the remaining molten glass.

Should you attempt to swirl when the enamel is not sufficiently melted, the tool will feel sluggish, stick in the enamel and drag up lumps of glass before it. The illustration, right, shows the result when a tool was drawn through a series of parallel molten opaque enamel threads.

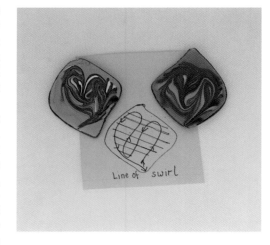

What happens when a piece is scrolled before becoming hot enough with its scrolling plan, together with the intended outcome.

Another point to be considered before swirling is that the piece must be supported underneath the whole stroke of the swirl. It is easy to tip it off a stilt, so try out the movement with a cold blank on its stilt first, positioned as it will be when in the kiln. Nevertheless, should it still tip up, all is probably not lost: just remove the tool and close the kiln briefly before taking the piece out. Do not try to loosen it from the stilt until it has solidified, then consider how it can be made good – marks on the back of the piece can be stoned off, repairs made if necessary and further scrolling could be added.

Mini-Project – Scrolling Pieces of Frit

1. Prepare a small oval with counter-enamel and a coat of soft white (or flux) on its front. (Soft enamels are suggested for your early pieces as they melt at lower temperatures and are therefore easier to execute.)

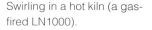

Swirling in a hot kiln (a gas-fired LN1000).

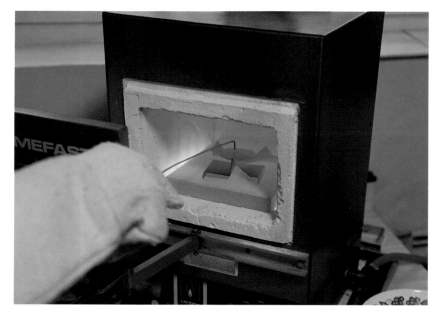

A scrolled frit brooch.

to leave stilt-marks on a domed swirled piece if it is then fired upside down, the piece can have the counter-enamel stuck on the back (gum, sprinkle, spray, resprinkle, respray and dry) and finally be fired with the swirling still uppermost. Another solution, for deeply domed pieces, is to counter-enamel lightly and rely on it hardly sticking to a mesh if swirled last.

Examine the four pieces in the photograph overleaf:

1. This piece was first counter-enamelled, given two coats of transparent blue and then scrolled on the stilt. It had three smallish lumps of soft white stuck in place, just touching, and was positioned in the kiln with the lumps away from the door. They expand and appear to merge on melting: the tool was placed into this white mass and simply pulled towards the door and lifted.
2. Here the method is similar, but three piles of soft white powder were used instead of the lumps – note the more defused outline. The tool was curled round at the bottom and small chips subsequently fired along this line.
3. The front was scrolled with the blank supported on a firing pad and counter-enamel was added afterwards. Bars of dark opaque green enamel were wet-laid across the paler-coloured fish, dried and the tool scrolled from the head to the tail, similar to 'feathering' when icing a cake.
4. A long double stilt afforded good support for this piece. A prepared, counter-enamelled blank had piles of opaque orange and green positioned. The tool was scrolled from the far end to the middle, the piece was turned round and re-heated, and the other end was then similarly scrolled.

2. Sprinkle lightly with a pale blue opaque enamel and position it across the larger stilt, so that short downwards strokes can be made without it tipping up. Place a few small pieces of opaque or transparent chips (frit) on top.
3. Heat until thoroughly molten and scroll three or four downward, stem-like, marks with the heated tool. Clean the tip and reheat between strokes if necessary.

Mini-Project – Several Experimental Scrolls

In order to get a better feel for using the tool and to learn more options available from this technique, try out the illustrated examples, or something similar, using whatever enamels you possess.

Swirled pieces normally need to be counter-enamelled before scrolling, but this could be done afterwards if the best overall support during scrolling calls for the work being laid directly onto a mesh or firing pad. However, as it is difficult not

Four simple scrolled pieces.

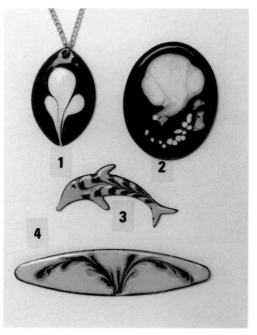

3. When really hot draw the scrolling tool down the centre of the cross and briefly close the door to heal any tool marks. The initial coat of soft enamel melts so readily that the action draws the surrounding enamel down, giving the overall effect.
4. Remove the excess firescale from the back (avoiding pickling to protect the soft enamel) and counter-enamel by gluing on an opaque enamel and firing on a stilt, right side up.

Swirling

Now for really 'swirling' the enamel, but again simple strokes create a better effect than scribbling.

Two swirled brooches – similarly scrolled with different-sized lumps.

PROJECT – A SCROLLED CROSS

This is very simple; any difficulty comes from its size (only 1½in or 3.5cm).

1. Enamel the front of the slightly domed cross with soft white.
2. Put on a transparent colour known to be hard enough to cause the bubbling-through effect.

PROJECT – TWO SWIRLED BROOCHES

1. Select two of the bigger round or diamond-shaped domed copper blanks (these shapes give more stability for swirling than an oval). Each will be fired on a large three-armed stilt. Plan your background colouring to complement some transparent

Scrolled crosses at different stages.

lumps. Use six smallish pieces, about ³⁄₁₆in (4mm) across, on one, and three or four larger lumps, about ⁵⁄₁₆in (8mm) across, on the other. In this instance they will all be placed approximately in the centre and comparing the two will show how much room differently sized lumps take up when they melt.

The left-hand brooch in the picture on page 56 had small lumps: two green, two blue and two different ambers on ocean blue. The other brooch had larger pieces: one green, one red and two amber lumps on Buckingham green. The lumps were swirled, from the middle, in a clover-leaf pattern.

2. Prepare each piece with a top coat of soft white and counter-enamel.
3. Test for stability on the large stilt – each section of the clover leaf will need to be swirled above a supporting arm of the stilt, all in a single continuous motion. Build your confidence by practising it in advance.
4. Sprinkle on the transparent colour, position on the stilt and add a small pile of soft white in the middle, nestling the lumps on top. This white helps to keep them from slipping, makes locating the centre easier when

Brooch prepared for swirling with four large lumps.

all the colours melt and adds to the appearance afterwards. (If you prefer, the overall colour can be fired in place before the lumps are glued on and the piece refired for swirling.)
5. Swirl each piece in a hot kiln, when really molten.

Swirling Taken Further

With practice, and the careful selection of colours, this technique can become quite

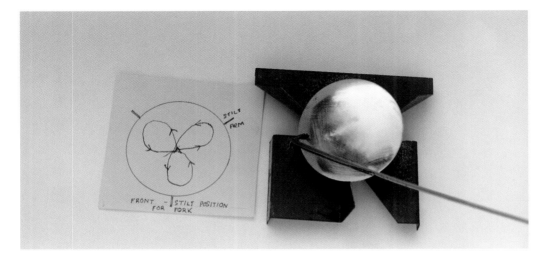

Testing to see if a piece will tip when swirled in accordance with planned movement.

Swirled fishes by Harry Morley.

Brooches incorporating melted non-enamelling glass and pewter backings.

sophisticated and artistic. It can also be done in a very controlled manner to depict flowers, fishes, and so on.

NON-ENAMELLING GLASS

It is unwise to try swirling in commercial bottle or stained glass, as they almost invariably have much higher melting temperatures than the enamels. However, small pieces can be slumped down, or melted into a ball by a lengthy firing, and then fused to a piece as shown in the photograph. One background design was stencilled and the other swirled through piles of 'opalescent' enamel; both had initial coats of soft white.

OPALESCENT ENAMELS

These enamels come in a range of colours and are semi-opaque, semi-transparent.

PEWTER MOUNTS

One satisfactory way to finish a regular-shaped piece is to back it by gluing on a

piece of thin pewter, just bigger than the copper. Use a petroleum-based contact glue, cover the base of any brooch pin, then tool over a thin, even lip onto the front.

SILVER FOIL

The sparkle and shine of your work can be heightened by fusing silver foil into the enamelling. Standard 'fine silver' foil is very thin, needs careful handling and is sold in squares, protected between layers

'Jazz' using silver foil for the trumpet and lightly fired decorative media as notes.

Cutting out a square of silver foil.

of tissue paper. It is normally cut, or even torn, into the required shape while still sandwiched either between this tissue or in a folded piece of thin paper on which the shape to be cut has been drawn. The foil itself is best handled with a paintbrush.

Pieces of foil can be inserted into a design: cutting with scissors will leave a distinct edge, tearing, a much softer one. Foil can also be used to completely cover a small piece of copper to give the effect of silver itself, but bigger shapes, especially domed ones, are best covered by many overlapping torn pieces that will fuse into a single silver surface when fired. You can save small off-cuts of foil for future use.

Firing silver directly over copper can trigger a damaging chemical reaction but, fortunately, the foil is always protected by fusing it to an existing smooth coat of enamel. Wetting the surface will help to position it and 'capillary action' will draw a drop of water, added with a brush to the edge of the foil, underneath it. The wet bits can be moved easily, but once in place they need to be pressed down with a tissue to remove as much trapped water and air as possible. Alternatively, you could try using the traditional method of putting a little saliva (known as 'jeweller's glue') onto the enamel. Always dry thoroughly before firing.

It can be difficult to see when the piece is hot enough to have fused. To help judge this, look for the stilt turning red, or add a few extra grains to a background colour near the foil and watch for this fusing. Should any foil lift, simply press it down with a palette knife or glass brush immediately it comes out of the kiln, and give the final layer of fused foil the protection of another coat of transparent enamel.

The colour of transparents over silver usually resembles that tested over white, but most reds need to be fired on top of a coat of flux to avoid unpredictable results

and the necessity of doing preliminary tests.

PROJECT – BROOCH WITH INSET BITS OF SILVER FOIL

1. Prepare an oval with one coat of flux and two coats of a transparent mid-green.

Positioning pieces of foil with a brush and water.

2. If the top is not really flat, stone it and flash fire.
3. Tear small pieces of foil and position them separately on the oval, moistening the edges with water.
4. Dry thoroughly and fire. Slight crinkling of the foil will create new reflective surfaces, adding to the final effect.
5. Cover the whole piece with a further coat of green.

PROJECT – PILLBOX WITH A SUNSET ON SILVER FOILED COPPER INSET

1. Check the fit of the copper inset for the pillbox, slightly rounding the corners.

Coloured foil mosaic brooch.

2. Give the square two really flat coats of flux, as well as counter-enamelling, and thoroughly clean its edges.
3. Cut a square of silver foil allowing for almost ¼in (5mm) overlap all round the copper.
4. Wet the copper (with water or saliva) and position the foil, pressing it down

Foil can be used to add accents to pictures and designs, as here on 'The Eucalyptus Tree'.

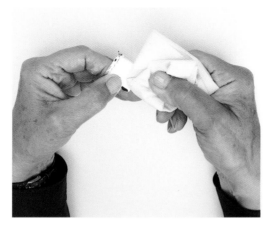

Using a tissue to expel water and air from underneath the foil.

with a tissue, working from the centre outwards, and turning it over the edge. Dry and fire.
5. Add a coat of flux to protect the silver.
6. Wet-lay a seaside sunset scene using transparent colours, dry and fire.
7. Fit the inset, filing its edge if necessary, and glue in place.

Pillbox with silver foiled lid.

GLAZES AND SUPERSOFT FLUX

Glazes

Any enamel can be given a transparent coating with a clear flux, and this appearance of a glass covering is particularly effective, as a final coat, over painting enamels, or when it is desired to even out the finished surface. Avoid using a flux that is harder than the underlying enamels and take care not to overfire a glaze – particularly a soft flux – that could burn out or cause the design to become slightly displaced.

Overfiring

The most noticeable effect of overfiring, in the majority of normal enamels, is for it to burn out, leaving a blackened matt edge or patch. This occurs when a piece is left too long in too hot a kiln, and can be controlled by the length of firing and the kiln temperature. Thin coats of enamel are more liable to burn out.

Supersoft Flux

Supersoft enamel melts at even lower temperatures than other 'soft' enamels, but will readily overflow onto adjacent areas. It is therefore used sparingly and not where it might run and spill onto the kiln floor. It should never be washed, put in acids or mixed with other enamels, and is only used as a final firing.

Its joy comes primarily from its tendency to take on golden, green and then brown colours, before losing its glazed surface, as it begins to burn out. It can also assimilate firescale into the design.

There is a special safety point to be remembered when using this enamel, because it has a more than average lead content. The grains are larger than usual and safe to handle provided there is no risk of ingesting them, but be particularly careful not to leave any on your hands or where they could contaminate food.

PROJECT – SUPERSOFT DISH

A dish is an ideal shape for trying this enamel because it will run down into the middle if applied too thickly or fired too much. However, the idea is to avoid this happening, merely to achieve interesting hues.

1. Counter-enamel in transparent green or brown and pickle the inside clear.
2. Shape a 'W' mesh to hold the dish level, while only touching the edge in a few places.
3. Dampen the inside of the dish with glue and sprinkle on a really thin coat of supersoft flux, taking care to spread it all over. Position on the mesh and dry.
4. Fire at a low-to-normal temperature (800–850°C), just until it glazes. Take

it out and let it cool sufficiently for you to see its true colour. Should the surface have burnt out where the enamel has been spread too thinly, add a little more supersoft and refire. (This will glaze over the dark areas of firescale, but not remove them.)

Supersoft fluxed dishes – the one underneath has fused, but it has not been left to develop the colours of the overfired dish on top.

5. Return the dish to the kiln and deliberately leave it for a longer firing, until browns appear, taking it out as soon as you achieve the colour you like.
6. The enamel has probably seeped onto the rim and is left there, but stone back any sharp or lumpy stilt marks.

PROJECT – SUPERSOFT AND FIRESCALE TRAY

1. Fire one good coat of counter-enamel on a tray or dish, allow it to cool naturally and tip off the loose firescale. The residual scale will provide random dark patches.
2. Gently apply glue, sprinkle with a thin coat of supersoft enamel, dry and

Induced Firescale

Controlled areas or lines of firescale can be encouraged by scraping back some of the first supersoft layer glued to cleaned copper, after it has dried and before giving it its first firing. Add a further sprinkling on top and refire.

Hand-fashioned supersoft dish with induced firescale lines.

fire until the fused tones look attractive.

3. Only add a repeat firing of supersoft if unglazed patches remain.

Two pieces with supersoft enamel fired over firescale.

Supersoft Enamel over other Enamelled Pieces

A supersoft glaze over other enamels can produce a defused finish and may introduce golden or green/brown colouring. Try this over some 'reject' pieces to see the effect.

PAINTING ENAMELS USED AS AN EMBELLISHMENT

Painting enamels can offer an ideal way to finish a piece enamelled in other techniques. They are, however, worked differently.

The enamel from pre-mixed tubes can be used directly, whereas the fine, powdered overglaze painting enamels need to be prepared by mixing with an oil-based medium or water – I suggest you use an oil, such as lavender oil or a proprietary brand, as this normally gives stronger colouring. The powder must be combined very thoroughly with the medium, using a palette knife on a piece of glass or glazed tile; but, ideally, finish the mixing with a muller on a piece of ground glass. (A muller is a small tool for grinding the grains of paint; a ground glass stopper from an old glass bottle or decanter can be used for this.) Aim for a really smooth paste, as soft as toothpaste, and only prepare what you need because a little goes a long way and it dries out quite quickly.

The metal for a painted enamel piece is prepared with at least two layers of enamel (most frequently white), stoned flat and flash-fired, but when paints are used to ornament an already enamelled piece, they can be applied on top of any substantially smooth glazed surface. They are quite low-firing so the underlying enamel need not be hard and a short firing at about 800°C is usually all that is required. Fire until the matt surface of the paint just turns shiny and be careful not to overfire. It is best to build up stronger colours in more than one firing of thin layers.

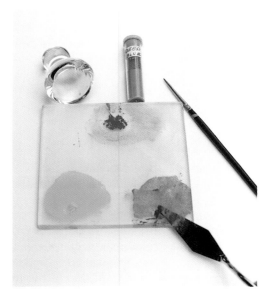

Mixing powdered enamel paints with a palette knife.

Painting enamels can be mixed like other artistic media to obtain intermediate colours, and their hues normally change very little with firing. However, testing is advisable when they are combined: this applies particularly to reds, which can be a little unreliable, both on their own or mixed with others; also they are always best put on last.

Apply the paint using small strokes with a very fine brush. Several areas of colour can be painted before each firing. Do not try to put it on too thickly or to superimpose coats until the underlying layer has been fired. The colour will spread slightly as it fuses, more so if it is excessively thinned or oily; in addition, it will sink into the surface if fired for too long.

When the paint is half dry its outline can be refined with the sharp tip of any tool. Leave it to dry out in no more than a gentle heat, but finally make sure it is absolutely dry by briefly holding it in the open mouth of the kiln to ensure no oily fumes are given off. Fire, let the piece cool slowly and add a flux glaze if you wish.

You can clean your oily paint brushes with washing-up liquid or methylated spirits.

Mini-Project – Test Piece for Coloured Enamel Paints

Try out your colours on a white enamelled plate and keep it for reference.

The flower dish in the photograph, right, was wet-laid over white enamel using the sgraffito method given in the next chapter, with added crushed orange enamel threads. Enamel paint was then used to finish it off. Green painting enamel was prepared and painted on quite thickly over the centre, inside the orange stamen tips. While this started drying the paint was diluted a little more

Test piece for basic painting enamel colours.

and the shaded grooves in the petals brushed in place. Once the central ring was half dry the radiating stalks of the stamens were depicted by carefully scraping off the enamel between them with the needle tool. When the dish had been dried and fired the thicker paint remained crisp and the thinner strokes on the petals more defused.

Flower dish finished with enamel paints.

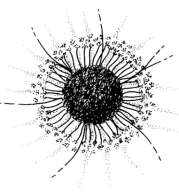

Enlarged detail of the centre of the flower to be painted and refined.

Mini-Project – Adding Paint to an Otherwise Completed Piece

In order to become more familiar with enamel paints, choose a small enamelled piece, even one that had been rejected, and use enamel paints to add shading or further features. You will find that shading is often best achieved by mixing the paint of a similar colour to the background, but in a darker hue; but be wary of adding too much black, as it tends to dominate mixes.

Paints are very useful when combined with other techniques. But if you want to be more ambitious, sketch an outline picture with a thin pastel colour, fire it and proceed with successive firings, in this order: background, mid-ground and detail.

Skilled work really requires further study, particularly before an artist enameller can produce the beautiful and intricate miniatures for which the technique is famed.

Painted enamel blue tit on silver by Janice Demaine.

7 Sgraffito and Liquid Enamels

This chapter is devoted to using the versatile liquid enamels, primarily with sgraffito, and offers the chance to take the techniques to quite an advanced, even experimental, level.

for decorative enamelling. They are lead-free but, nevertheless, form an ideal foundation for the leaded jewellery enamels, and are fired in the same traditional way.

Supplies

Most suppliers stock liquid whites, while W. G. Ball also manufacture and sell a full range of opaque colours and a flux in their 'wet process' range. Experiment with one of the whites first, but if the style appeals you may well want to try out the ideas for fluxes or colours. A variety of copper blanks can be used but many projects are designed for bowls, dishes and, later, pictures.

These enamels are ideally suited for a more controlled and advanced sgraffito work than that introduced in Chapter 4, and there are specific whites or fluxes that make it possible to do exceptionally fine line drawing; choose them if this is your forte. You only need the needle tool and straw, supplemented by a pointed orange stick, all used to inscribe your design into a dry (or rather, substantially dry) coating of liquid enamel.

'Pitstone Windmill' – liquid white enamel, sgraffitoed with transparent colouring.

LIQUID ENAMELS

These provide another variation in the manufacture and presentation of enamel, this time with very finely ground grains suspended in a liquid base. Commercially, they are sprayed onto metal to achieve enduring smooth finishes, as on a cooking stove, but they also can be used

Liquid Whites

Those sold as liquids, prepared ready to use, are probably best, but I have found Ball's 'Steel White' and their 'Wet Process White (10099)' most suitable for intricately drawn work.

They are pre-mixed to the consistency of pouring (i.e. single) cream and should be used at this thickness. Try not to let the liquor evaporate in the pot: if it does, thicken or dry, then dilute it with purified or distilled water. Always stir thoroughly before using.

Application to the Copper

Liquid enamels can only be applied evenly if the copper is scrupulously clean. This can be ensured if it is prepared as usual and then given a final scouring with a little of the enamel itself.

Small pieces can be dipped into the enamel; the enamel can be poured on and the excess tipped off; or the enamel can be painted on. Only a thin coating is required, and applying the layer in the right thickness is vital. Achieve this by using the enamel at the correct consistency (pouring cream) and then leaving on just sufficient for the copper to still show through, as a very faint pink. When it dries it should look white, completely covering up the metal; if the dry coating looks granular, with the copper still just visible, the liquid has been thinned too much. It must be absolutely dry before firing.

SGRAFFITO

When a design is scratched through a coat of dry, unfired, liquid white, to expose the bare copper, firing will glaze the white enamel and leave firescale wherever the sgraffito marks have been made.

Scraping away the liquid white is best done when the coat has virtually dried; that is, when the grains easily loosen, are powdery and readily tip off. However, if the enamel is dried artificially, or left on a really hot day, the layer tends to cake onto the copper and becomes hard to scratch

loose. When dried on an ordinary, dampish English day or in a slightly steamy kitchen it will retain just enough moisture. Nevertheless, a baked-dry piece can be 're-humidified' by leaving it, for about fifteen minutes, under a damp cloth held clear of the work by placing it under an inverted kitchen sieve.

Home-made 'humidifier' for over-dry coatings.

Thickness and Firing

Gentle strokes are the best way to scratch out the marks without the enamel flaking off the unfired coat. If the layer is applied on the thick side, repeat the strokes until enough copper is exposed; but if the coat is too thick the enamel edges can become lumpy or even roll back on firing. However, the surface of a thick top layer can be carefully pared back, and varying the depth of the coat can be used to create different effects.

In normal circumstances the piece should only be left in the kiln until it has glazed. Finally, if the white starts to burn out unexpectedly quickly, or go green, the layer may have been too thin.

Doing a few tests and noting the results is the best way to understand the possibilities of this technique. Try it out on some small pieces of copper, gently scribing with the needle tool, then widening the line with the orange stick.

Mini-Project – Tests for Sgraffito in Liquid White

1. Find a plastic lid (from a food container with a slight rim) to use as a drying tray.
2. Thoroughly clean both sides of four pieces of copper, finishing off by scouring with a little of the enamel on a damp cloth. You can save waste enamel for scouring, but never return powdered enamel to the liquid in the pot

Scouring with the liquid enamel.

3. Make sure the liquid white is well mixed and at the right consistency.
4. Either dip one of the pieces of copper in the enamel pot, or pour it over both sides while firmly holding a corner of the copper with finely pointed tweezers. Let the excess enamel run back into the pot, and finally encourage more to drip off by tapping either the edge of the copper, or the top of the tweezers, with the side of the palette knife, until there is only the required quite thin (very slightly pink) covering when the piece is held horizontally.

Tapping to encourage excess liquid enamel to drip off.

5. Gently prop the piece, level and right side up, across the rim of the plastic lid, where air can circulate all round, and let it dry naturally. Once dry the covering is remarkably durable if handled with care, and any excessive thickening of the enamel on the back, where it touched the lid, can be pared off.
6. Your first test piece should have the correct thickness of enamel. Scribe 'MEDIUM' (for thickness) and 'L/MED FIRE' (for a low to medium firing) and fire it in a kiln at a normal temperature (about 830°C) until it glazes smooth.

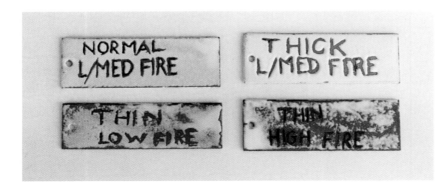

Some test pieces for liquid white.

Note that the owl in the photograph has fine lines sgraffitoed with the needle and has had a low firing. It will require finishing with a further coat of flux or light brown to seal and glaze the firescale marks.

The polar bear was drawn in a relatively thin layer, and its outline was widened with the tip of an orange stick; the ice flow behind it was both thinned and marked with the straw tool. After a low firing, more white was selectively brushed on top, to make the bear and some of the ice whiter; the bear was rescribed before the piece was fired again. It needs a final glazing with flux.

7. Repeat the procedure on another piece, but this time leave a little more enamel to fire a 'THICK – L/MED FIRE' test.

8. Prepare two more pieces with the coating diluted slightly with additional water. These are for 'THIN – LOW FIRE' and 'THIN – HIGH FIRE' tests, the former being removed from the kiln as soon as the enamel fuses, the latter left longer until it starts burning out.

Keep these pieces for future reference.

Mini-Project – Trial Pieces: an Owl and a Polar Bear

Cover one or two copper blanks in liquid white and practice sgraffito.

TIPS

- If you cool the hot fired piece in water you may loose the dark lines from the firescale.
- Dipping the copper into the liquid white covers both sides and makes specific counter-enamelling unnecessary.
- An unfired coat of liquid enamel need not be fired at once, but should be protected against accidental marking.
- Avoid the temptation to blow the loose powder away, unless you can control exactly where the enamel goes.

Sgraffito used simply, with varied intensities of white.

Transferring a Design into the Dry Coat of Liquid White

The robust nature of the unfired coat makes it easy to repeat a design in the enamel using a traced template, held on top of the dry white layer. The needle tool is then scratched round the outline, and key points in the central design marked through pin holes in the paper. These templates can be saved and used several times; they can also be adapted to fit the contours of dishes.

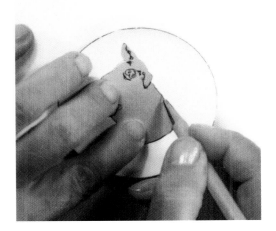

Template being used. Note that the position of the pig's eye, nose, etc., are also marked.

Sprinkled colouring used for a wren dish.

Colouring Sgraffitoed Pieces

Lines drawn and fired into a white base can simplify subsequent colouring with transparent enamels. Sprinkling a light colour over the piece will tint the white, but hardly be noticeable over the brown scale lines (as in the sky behind the windmill sails in the photograph on page 65).

The template used to copy the wren in the picture, right, was also used as a stencil while the background blue sky was sprinkled over the dish, including the freehand scribing of the tree. After this was fired, the wren was coloured by fawn being sprinkled onto glue, spread all over the centre; once it was dry, the part outside the bird's silhouette was scraped loose and tipped off. Take care that a layer, sprinkled onto glue with the intention of cutting it back to an underlying line, does not obliterate that line.

Wet-laying the colours is often a more attractive option, but the two methods can be combined, a sprinkled pastel background being supplemented by wet-laid features.

Wet-laying the entire piece is time-consuming and cannot be hurried. You must first wash all the required covering enamels. Wipe glue over the fired liquid white, then lay all the enamels, working systematically across the piece. Remember that moisture control is the key to successful wet-laying: never let the newly laid layer of grains dry out where you are working but, on the other hand, if you get the piece too wet the grains will be uncontrollable and will intermingle in the resulting puddle. Have a small pot of distilled water and a tissue on hand to add or take water out of your work or tools.

Once you have completed one area of colour, wash out your brush or straw tool in the distilled water, letting the grains fall to the bottom. Then start on the next colour, carefully laying it alongside the first area while this is still damp. If the initial part has dried too much it will suck water from the new colour – you will soon find that this second area cannot be laid smoothly unless all those it touches have an equal water content. (Only use the spray very sparingly, as it dampens indiscriminately.)

At least two fired layers of colour are needed for most wet-laid designs.

PROJECT – SGRAFFITOED 'ROCKING SEA HORSE' DISH

1. Trace or photocopy the sea horse and cut out the outer shape for a template. Mark the position of the eye, hand/fin and the line of the neck at the base of the crest, with pin holes, the fewer the better. (Try highlighting the pin-

Design for the 'Rocking Sea Horse'.

prick points on the template with a marker pen or circle ⊗.) Less confident artists could cut the template to include the front waves, so they can draw round this, then cut the waves off and re-use it to add the line between the animal and these waves.

2. Counter-enamel a suitably sized dish once, pickle and clean. This will prevent firescale forming every time it is fired, and it can be supported on a 'W' mesh whenever the front requires firing.

3. Stir up the liquid white, making sure it is at the consistency of pouring cream. Pour some into the dish, tipping and rotating it until it is entirely covered, then pouring off the excess by tapping the edge of the dish until enough has run off.

4. When it is virtually dry, position the template, draw round it with the needle tool and mark the pinpricks firmly enough to be seen. Remove the template and make sure that the marks do not get lost by suggesting the lines they indicate – do this before tipping off the loosened powder as they could become covered over.

5. Draw in the eyes, fin and scales, etc., and add the secondary waves and clouds. Tip off all the loose enamel and widen the main lines of the sea horse and the front waves with an orange stick; these last lines should be completely clear, but if a fine dusting of powder is left on other lines it can give them an attractive sheen.

    Mistakes can be difficult to correct at this stage, so I suggest that you do not attempt to add more liquid enamel until it has been fired once, then make good in an additional firing.

6. Fire until it is glazed.

7. Decide on the colour for the sea and sky (aqua and crystal are used in the

Sgrafittoed dish coloured by combining wet laying with a sprinkled background.

12. Stone off any stilt marks, invert the dish and give the underside a second coat.
13. Clean the edge, possibly varnishing it to prevent future tarnishing.

OTHER WET PROCESS ENAMELS

These are used similarly, but many cannot be sgraffitoed as finely. The opaque colours usually require two or more coats, making them less suitable for sgraffito, and the flux must be applied quite thinly or it will remain cloudy. (The relatively new flux LF98 has some unique properties and there are more details about it on page 77.) In addition, liquid enamels can be mixed together or laid on top of one another.

Crackle Enamels

These are liquid enamels that are specifically prepared to crack, producing a sort of crazy paving look, when put on top of a coat of ordinary enamel. The cracks are more pronounced on curved surfaces and can be encouraged with the odd needle stroke.

This crackle effect will probably occur if any liquid enamel is put on top of an ordinary enamel.

illustrated example) and get them ready to sprinkle. Use the sea horse template as a stencil after adding a tag to make it easy to lift. Hold it in place on the dish with a finger while covering the outer area with gum, then quickly sprinkle the blues, fading them both as they merge on the skyline and making them deeper at the top and bottom. This has to be done quickly, while the glue is still wet, although you can spray and continue sifting in the knowledge that if the stencil is in place it will also get wet.

8. Carefully remove the stencil. The glue that has got onto its edge should hold most of the stray grains in place; the rest are tipped off.
9. When the blues have dried, use the straw to loosen any that remain on the sea horse and, if you like, to give the near waves white tops. Tip off the loose enamel and fire until fused.
10. Wet-lay the sea horse (gold and orange), giving it a black and opal white eye. Add the headland on the skyline (pale grey).
11. Fire on further layers of colouring as required.

Testing and Ideas for Taking the Sgraffito Methods Further

This technique offers infinite possibilities to be explored, some of which are suggested here. Test out your ideas, keep your trial pieces, and notes on the results, carefully for future reference. They may be able to be combined with the following variations.

MIXING LIQUID FLUX AND LIQUID WHITE

These two liquid enamels can be used side-by-side, or mixed together in a single coat, and then sgraffitoed. The main advantage is that it facilitates a wide variety of tone, from white to that of clear fluxed copper. The main disadvantage comes from the fact that both enamels appear white before being fired! Therefore careful planning and working is more essential than ever.

An easy way to measure enamels to be mixed is to have them at the correct consistency for use and then count out level spoonfuls using a small plastic tea- or salt spoon.

The liquid enamels are still spread in a normal thickness and, as in wet-laying, care is needed to ensure that any already positioned area is wet enough not to suck water from the newly applied enamel. This is best done by keeping the plate damp by spraying it lightly whenever it dries out, and laying the next area almost up to where they meet before pushing it right up to the join, if the design requires them to touch. (This dividing line is often planned for sgraffitoing later, so ends up as a neat mark.)

Suitable Subjects

Pictures or designs for this technique need to be simple and I suggest you start by using only three or four tones: liquid white, liquid flux and two intermediate mixes, these being equal parts of white and flux, that gives a rather translucent white; and 1:3 (white:flux) where the copper will clearly show through as a watery, milky colour. Plan it in detail on a drawing, on the same scale as the chosen copper plate.

Start by putting the liquid white over the major areas where this is wanted. Dry and cut it back, using a template or templates, to exactly where it is needed. It may help to fix the copper to a piece of board temporarily with some bits of double-sided sticky tape, then fix the template(s) in the same way so they can be folded back over the plate, accurately positioned. Instead of double-sided sticky tape you could use a short length of normal tape, rolled sticky side out, and press the copper well home. This will subsequently release the piece easily.

PROJECT – COLOURED PICTURE OF KING PENGUINS, INITIALLY SGRAFFITOED IN LIQUID FLUX AND WHITE

1. Counter-enamel and pickle a 3½in × 2⅜in (8.5cm × 6.5cm) plate and clean it thoroughly. This is large enough to try out the method, but can be scaled up and elaborated.
2. Cut the templates and position them, and the plate, as illustrated. A few pencilled marks on the plate make useful guidelines for the area to be covered, but must be rubbed out once the excess enamel is scratched off.
3. Prepare the liquid enamels and a 1:3 white:flux mixture.
4. Apply liquid white to extend over more than the areas where it is wanted: on the bottom section (snow and the standing birds) and on the strip for the mountains. Leave to dry. If you want to remove the plate from the board temporarily when applying a section of liquid enamel, you must reposition it accurately.
5. Fold the bottom (blue) template back over the plate and sgraffito the upper

sky
(1:3 mix)

mountains
(white)

water
(flux)

snow and birds
(white)

Drawing for
sgraffitoing king
penguins in an
Antarctic setting.

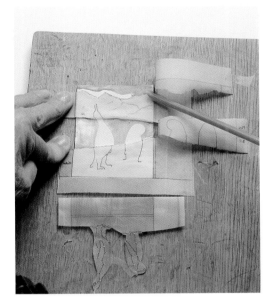

Templates positioned for sgraffitoing the liquid
enamel mixes.

outlines of the birds. Replace this
template with the yellow one, dividing
up the scenic background; and
scratch the lines for the top and bottom
of the mountains, and the dividing
line between the foreground and
the icy water, in the same way, being
careful not to take them behind the
birds. Scrape off and remove the
excess white enamel from the plate.

6. Check that the prepared 1:3 mix has
not dried and spray the partly covered
plate damp, while shielding the
folded-back templates. Add the 1:3
(sky), laying it a little thicker at the
top (which will make it whiter when
fired) and leaving it fractionally short
of the mountain tops. This skyline
will be lightly sgraffitoed when it is
dry.

7. Lay liquid flux onto the remaining
middle strip of copper in the same

way, on either side of the standing bird to represent the icy water. Take it just up to the mountains and down to the foreground snow, and add touches of the 1:3 to indicate ice flows.

The fired plate showing the variety of tones in the sgraffitoed background.

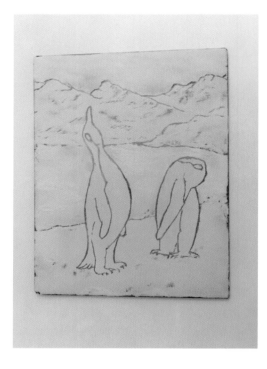

Overall whiteness of a sgraffitoed, unfired liquid white and flux plate.

8. When the plate has dried, reposition the penguin template to reinforce their outline, locate and scratch in the lower details (feet) and add their markings. The side template can be used to relocate and sgraffito the scenic background dividing lines. Add the shady places in the mountains.
9. Lift off the board and fire. It is only now that the flux element of the coat becomes transparent.

Improved picture based on the simpler project piece.

10. Wet-lay the washed coloured enamels and flux. The penguins' feather colouring was achieved using opal white, pigeon and a 'transparent' black, with a little orange and gold in the neck plumage and beak (*see* the photograph on page 74). Put flux over the white mountains, snow and water, and blue for the sky, trying to make the whole layer as flat as possible before firing. Any slightly lumpy places could be stoned back (under running water) before the second layer is laid. The side of the plate can be tapped to level out the newly wet-laid flux, but beware of causing a loss of definition in carefully laid adjacent colours by injudicious agitation.

11. Shadows, footmarks, etc., are added on the second wet-laying. Alternatively, use enamel paints.

12. Mount and frame.

Lustre was added to this geometric dish by fusing inset patches of silver foil onto the fired liquid white before the colours are applied.

A Purely Tonal Picture

This picture, 'The Medieval Village', uses liquid flux and white only. Initially the liquid enamels were applied similarly to the penguins and fired onto the plate. Some small white details (such as sheep, figures and the cart) were added in a second firing. A thin coat of well-washed normal flux was then sifted and fired over the whole picture.

Manipulating Wet Liquid Enamels with the Needle Tool

Liquid enamels, including coloured ones, can be manipulated while wet with the needle tool, as in the photograph below. The billowing smoke surrounding the phoenix capitalizes on the readiness of steel white to intermix with wet-process flux when still wet, whereas other coloured wet-process enamels retain their definition better when intermingled in the same way.

Foiled phoenix, in flames of liquid enamels manipulated while wet.

The phoenix was cut out of silver foil and fused to a patch of liquid flux, pre-fired onto the centre of the plate. Transparent gold was wet-laid and fired precisely over the foil, and all the firescale that had formed on the rest of the plate was removed. Liquid flux was applied thinly to the smoky area and sprayed to make it even wetter. The needle tool was used in a swirling motion to disperse drops of steel white placed into the flux, and the wet plate jogged to add to the intermixing. While this was allowed to dry slightly, patches of liquid yellow and red were liberally placed round (but not over) the bird and drawn out with the needle to represent the flames. More was added as required and the reds taken into the smoke, until the whole plate was covered. The plate was resprayed whenever necessary.

You can cut straw shovels for each liquid enamel colour, and use them to scoop it from the pots and pull it off with the needle tool. Thus only the needle needs cleaning after each colour is applied.

Two coats were necessary for the flames (especially the red), but superimposing the colours precisely is not essential. Finally the firewood and the outline of the bird were added in liquid black, with the lines refined when they had dried. 'Crackle' was avoided by not covering the leaded gold enamel.

OTHER USES FOR WET-PROCESS COLOURED ENAMELS

Counter-Enamelling

Put a layer on the back of a piece and let it dry before working on the front. Firing both simultaneously saves time.

Three-Dimensional Work

The ability of these enamels to coat the copper can provide an ideal way to enamel awkwardly shaped copper pieces.

Three-dimensional picture worked with liquid enamels on thin copper.

Wet-Process Enamelled Pillboxes

Fire a layer of 'wet process ground coat', followed by two or three coats of coloured enamel, onto a copper box and its lid, before gluing them into the gilt hinge rings. Each coat is applied by dipping into the enamel, putting on an even covering, drying and firing.

Pill boxes using wet process enamels.

LATHAM'S LIQUID FLUX LF98

This flux has recently become available, it is capable of producing a beautifully clear finish and can be sgraffitoed in incredible detail, but it is not the easiest to use. However, anyone who enjoys fine pen-work should find mastering it very rewarding and I have had success by observing the following points, that are specific to LF98, as opposed to other liquid enamels:

- Only use immaculate copper, as the slightest mark will show.
- Always stir the enamel thoroughly immediately before use; this may take some effort and time as it readily cakes at the bottom of the pot. (The clarity has been obtained at the cost of prolonging the suspension of the extremely fine grains in their liquid.) You could keep a plain stainless steel knife specially for stirring up liquid enamel and 'spooning' it onto the plate.
- Maintain and use the enamel in a more runny state than hitherto.
- Its layer should consequently be thinner than those you have used before and soon dries. Work as quickly as possible: stir, spoon on enough enamel, spread, remove excess, hold level for a final tapping, and leave to dry flat.
- The plate should look pink while wet, with any sgraffito underneath showing clearly. When dry, the marks are almost obliterated by a white coat.
- Any dry part looking really white is too thick and will remain cloudy on firing. However, excess can be carefully pared, or wiped, off.
- Coats of LF98 are not robust, need careful handling and are too delicate for templates to be used safely.
- Sgraffito, when absolutely dry, with the needle tool first. Small mistakes can be covered by sieving on some of the powdered enamel, pushing flat with a clean, smooth, rounded tool and gently blowing off any excess.
- Never return dried-out grains to the pot.
- It is important that the first firing is only the minimum that will fuse the enamel. Use a moderately heated kiln (800–850°C). If you can see inside you will notice that the piece will turn almost black before going brown as it fuses – take it out as soon as its colour begins to lighten, otherwise the very thin coat will start to burn out.
- Build up the thickness of enamel with a second, and then a third, thin protective coat of LF98, firing each for a little longer. The underlying copper will successively change colour from bronze to rich pink and on to a golden colour.
- Some of the finest marks will be lost with each firing. Plan for this and if you want particularly dark lines repeat the sgraffito in the second coat, allowing the firescale to build up.

Sgraffito picture using only LF98 liquid flux.

Suitable Subjects

An engraver's style of drawing is ideal for this process, but intricate. It is, therefore, sensible to try both the sgraffito and the firing of successive coats first, on something both small and simple.

Trial pieces for LF98.

Mini-Project – Trial Piece for Sgraffito in LF98 Flux

Choose whatever suits your taste and skill – two alternatives are suggested, both using varying width of lines. The colour of the dragonfly typifies this enamel when it has only been sgraffitoed and fired once, while the lighter overall hue of the picture comes from a second firing, with the darkest parts being re-sgraffitoed, and finally a third coat fused on top.

These pieces do not necessarily require any further colouring, although this flux can also be used in all the ways described for other liquid enamels. Read through the guidelines again before having a go.

PROJECT – BROWNSEA ISLAND CHURCH – SGRAFFITOED IN LF98

This picture was actually planned from a watercolour sketch but I used photographs for further reference. Why not try a picture of your choice instead? A black and white photocopy of a painting or colour photograph helps in planning the depth of tones for a sgraffito drawing.

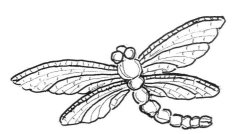

Drawings for trial pieces using LF98 flux.

Working drawing marked in centimetres.

1. Make a pen-and-ink drawing to scale with the proposed 2 × 2½in (5 × 6.5cm) copper plate. This makes it easier to subsequently position and copy the main lines and angles accurately.

2. Counter-enamel the plate, clean the front and coat with LF98.

3. Mark the key points in the enamel. Anyone apprehensive about this could cut out a 'frame' in thick or double corrugated paper, as in the diagram, so it can be fixed round the plate in such a way that a ruler can be used, laid across it, clear of the plate. The frame can include measurement markings.

4. Outline the main drawing with the needle tool. Add the detail, remembering that the piece will be fired three times, thereby losing some of the finest detail. The grass and sunny side of the building contain a few fine short lines only, whereas the shaded stonework has more concentrated marks. Once the initial work is done throughout the drawing, and the loosened enamel removed, the main lines are overdrawn again to give them emphasis.

5. Fire the piece at a moderate temperature – only until the fused flux looks a dusky pink. Give it a second coating and carefully resgraffito the darkest areas (the yew, Scots pine and doorway, etc.), removing the flux but not the firescale.

6. Refire the plate at the same temperature until the colour is fractionally lighter.

7. Glaze the entire picture with a final coat of LF98, firing until the desired tone is just achieved.

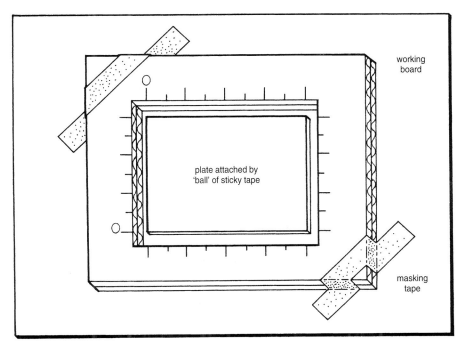

working board

plate attached by 'ball' of sticky tape

masking tape

Protective cardboard frame for sgrafittoing work.

'Brownsea Island Church', LF98 liquid flux used for an engraving style of sgraffito drawing.

8 Repoussé and Enamelling on Thin Copper

The final techniques covered in detail are those using copper, thin enough to be easily cut and shaped by hand before enamelling. This allows a great freedom of three-dimensional design, including creating undulating surfaces. Varying the depth of transparent enamels also brings changes in the intensity of colouring and gives some of the sparkle and range of tones usually only obtainable from engraving and other skilled ways of cutting into the surface of the copper before it is enamelled.

millimetres. At 0.06mm it is very malleable, but it can still be worked at 0.15mm, even though it is then far more rigid. Stiffness can be reduced by annealing, but already softened metal can be bought and, because it is frequently used in craft work, good local art and craft shops will normally stock or obtain it.

REPOUSSÉ

Repoussé (from the French *pousser*, 'to push out') is done by forcing the metal up from the underside, then continuing to work it from alternate sides; the technique is similar to that frequently used on pewter. With either metal, it is worked on a soft surface, yet one which will provide enough support for it to be indented by a tool being pressed down on the top.

Copper Foil

The thin copper sheet used for repoussé is sometimes referred to as 'shim' and is only about 0.004in (0.1mm) thick, with measurements usually just given in

Repoussé picture, 'Eastern Pheasant'.

Tools for Repoussé

Specialist modelling tools are ideal but not essential, as everyday substitutes are readily at hand. The minimum required are a reasonably pointed 'tracer' to draw lines and a 'modelling spatula' or 'modelling tool' for raising rounded areas. Start with an empty fine ballpoint pen: use the tip for lines and its rounded top to mould curves. (A thumb nail is an excellent, readily available alternative, tool.) However, a variety of shapes is best, and some alternatives are shown in the photograph below, along with those purpose-made for modelling in clay, pewter or parchment.

Tools and alternatives for working copper foil (shim).

You will also want a working fine ballpoint pen, a pair of strong pointed tweezers, a craft knife and some smallish scissors – embroidery ones are excellent (they need to be quiet sharp, but cutting the copper will blunt them in time).

Prepare a soft pad to work on, at least 4in (10cm) square, by placing a piece of felt on top of several sheets of blotting paper or non-shiny newspaper. For a more permanent solution buy an embossing pad or replace the newspaper with a sample-sized square of piled linoleum-type (flotex) floor covering. Try out your tools on a scrap of copper foil, working methodically over the area to be tooled, and find how much pressure is required to mark and shape the copper you have chosen.

Suitable Designs for Pictures

Repoussé designs tend to consist of bold and colourful shapes, and ideas for subjects can be gleaned from many sources. Bear in mind that small moulded and enamelled pieces of copper foil have considerable strength, but anything more than 2½in (6cm) across is liable to warp or crack; however, several pieces may be safely combined, by fusing or sticking them together, and collages can be built up. Also, it is normally desirable to avoid any vulnerable edges sticking out from a picture by bending them down or under; this has the added bonus of adding to the strength of the piece. The rounded forms of natural objects make them particularly suitable. Select your frame or mount before finalizing the size and positioning of the pieces within a design.

The following project illustrates how to prepare and enamel copper for repoussé, and is planned to fit into an everyday embroidery frame, backed by stiff card covered with paper or felt.

PROJECT – A REPOUSSÉ VIOLA

Shaping and cutting the five petals in three pieces will simplify assembling them – they can be folded into place after enamelling.

Design drawings for small repoussé viola picture.

1. Copy the separate parts onto thin tracing or greaseproof paper.
2. Temporarily fix the tracing over the copper with some sticky tape, allowing a margin of ⅛in (0.5cm) round each piece. Retrace each part by pressing quite hard with a fine ball-point pen over the pad – the inking of the line will remind you which parts have been redrawn. The tip must leave an indentation in the copper.
3. Remove the tracing and rescribe the outline, using the empty ballpoint this time so as not to mark the copper. Add the leaf veins – the marks will remain even if the leaf is subsequently raised.
4. Give shape to the petals by turning the copper over on the pad and using a rounded tool to dome each one slightly. Mould the leaves, working from both sides of the metal.
5. On the right side, over a hard and flat surface, press down the edges of the petals and leaves to level their outlines, and cut them out along this line. Carefully use tweezers to remove any distortions made during cutting, while turning the edges of the leaves slightly downwards and crimping them back where they indent.

Tracing to indent the copper from the leaf design.

Levelling out the edge of a raised leaf.

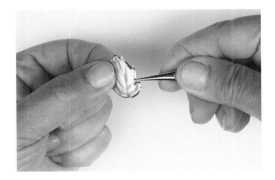

Using tweezers to crimp back leaf edge.

using a bristle or glass brush (an old soft toothbrush or bristle oil paint-brush will do).

9. Counter-enamel all but the smallest pieces, pickle and clean. Alternatively, this can be done, firing the underside simultaneously with the top, using the glue, sprinkle and spray method, or just painting on liquid enamel. Dry and turn over.

10. Put on a thin layer of gum on the top and sprinkle with enamel. This is probably easiest to do by holding the pieces with the tweezers by parts that will eventually be covered up (such as the extra bar linking pairs of petals, or the end of the stalks).

11. Once dry, fire the separate pieces on a firing pad and file or stone the edges smooth. Repeat where necessary.

12. Assemble the flower by bending the pairs of petals into place, folding under the tab sticking up from the bottom lobe and positioning them together on a firing pad with the bent linking strips hidden behind the single petal. Once positioned, add a small triangle of wet-laid opaque yellow/cream in the centre (covering up any crack in the enamel made when

The completed repoussé viola.

Sifting the enamel onto a leaf.

6. The stalks are virtually straight, with a square cross section, and made long enough for the end to fit underneath the flower or leaf. Crease the foil along the dotted line, cut them out (three times their finished width – *see* the diagram on page 82) and bend down the sides over a ruler edge.

7. Check that the pieces are correctly sized for later assembly within the frame. This technique has the added bonus that bits can be repositioned easily, even replaced.

8. Before enamelling the blue flower and green leaves, clean the copper by pickling, then gently scour both sides,

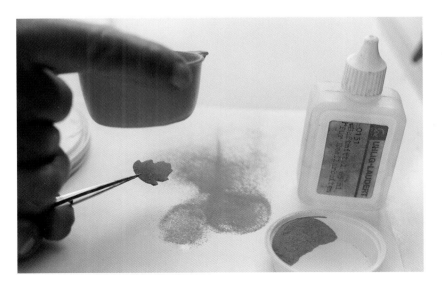

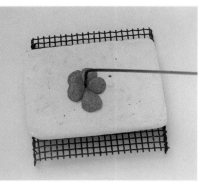

Flower head, assembled and being fused together.

folding). Dry and fire, and while still molten use the scrolling tool to gently press the middle together, so the flower head is fused into one piece. (Pieces for firing can be held in place by sticking ordinary steel pins into the pad alongside the edge of the metal.)

13. Any piece that will touch the backing card can be glued on directly, provided this will not show. Pieces whose underside is concave will need to be attached by small hinges cut from thin card and used similarly to mounting postage stamps. Cut the card hinges and glue several, by one arm, to the underside of each leaf and flower. Narrow hinges can be inserted on the bottom ends of the stalks.

14. Prepare a suitable rigid backing card and assemble it in the frame. Position and stick the enamelled pieces in place, preferably with a glue that retains a little elasticity (such as Uhu), and be liberal with the glue inside the hinges. Lightly weigh down the pieces until the glue dries.

card tag

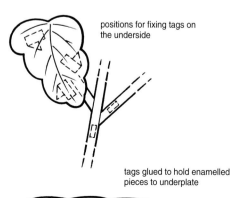

positions for fixing tags on the underside

tags glued to hold enamelled pieces to underplate

Positioning the fixing hinge tags and glue to mount repoussé pieces.

Additional Hints and Ideas for Repoussé Enamelling

- The copper pieces can still be trimmed with scissors after covering with a single thin coat of enamel, but these edges should be hidden or the piece refired.
- Extra height can be given by superimposing moulded pieces, such as in the big tree of the 'Teddy Bear's Picnic'.

Repoussé picture, 'Teddy Bears' Picnic'.

- This picture also incorporates cut paper backing and is recessed in the frame, to compensate for the extra height, by hiding strips of mounting card behind the flange of the frame where glass might otherwise be held.
- Pieces can be gently pressed together in the kiln, with a palette knife, to make them fuse firmly.
- Sgraffitoing into an initial coat of liquid flux adds emphatic lines that can follow the moulded grooves, as in the pheasant in the photograph on page 80.
- Electrical copper wire is nearly always pure enough to enamel after removing any lacquer, but always test first.
- Cutting irregular shapes out with the point of a craft knife can simultaneously push the jagged edges downwards.

- A liquid flux coat makes a good base for covering the copper with silver foil. Painting enamel is used, as well as the foil, on the wings of the fairy in the photograph below – which is itself fused to the 'pupil of the eye' (the underside of a flat-bottomed dish).

Repoussé picture, 'An Ox-eye Daisy Fairy'.

- Odd ends of wallpaper provide a useful source of backing paper for repoussé pictures.

REPOUSSÉ BROOCHES

Surprisingly robust brooches can be made from this thin copper, provided they are small, rounded in shape and have no projections that could either break off or snag material. They must be given at least three coats of enamel on both sides and further strength is then added by the judicious placing and gluing of the brooch pin, using the longest that can be hidden from view. Varying and increasing the modelling is another way to make the piece stronger.

PROJECT – A REPOUSSÉ BROOCH

This sea horse design is an adaptation of the one used for the sgraffito dish, and its colouring can be selected to match different outfits.

1. Trace the sea horse design, copy and scribe it in the copper.
2. Raise the body and crest from the back of the metal.
3. Reverse the copper and redraw the lines with the fine ball tool before raising each segment again. This should lift these internal lines slightly and partially dome the whole piece.

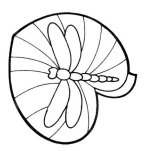

4. Run a wide tool round the outline on a flat surface to straighten the piece, and cut just outside the line.
5. The hole in the curl of the tail is pushed through from the front and the copper outline is given a distinct curl downwards with the tweezers as the shape is refined.
6. Clean the copper, dip into liquid enamel flux and allow to dry.
7. Sgraffito the indented lines on the front with the needle, widen them with an orange stick and fire on a pad. File the edges smooth.
8. Apply some liquid enamel to the back, dry and ensure the front is clean.

Repoussé brooches: initial fluxed coat and finished sea horses.

Sea horse and other brooch patterns.

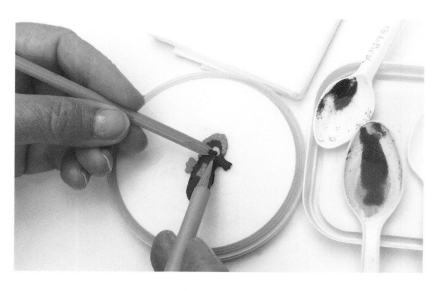

Adding the pupil of the eye to the wet-laid brooch top.

Alternative Brooches

Make a brooch of the dragonfly on a lily leaf by preparing the dragonfly, covering it with foil, colouring it and then fusing it flat onto an enamelled leaf. Try other brooches, preferably of your own design. They should easily pass the washing machine test, that is, come out unscathed if inadvertently left on a garment being washed!

Foiled dragonfly incorporated in repoussé brooch.

9. Select and wash your transparent colours, as well as small quantities of opalescent white and black for the eye.

10. In order to prepare the top and fire the enamel on both sides at the same time, try putting a little glue on the front of the piece, placing it on a small plastic lid and wet-laying the top. This will allow you to turn the copper, without moving the piece, while you put on the colours and the eye (the black pupil is probably best inserted last, by pulling a little off a loaded straw into the wet white of the eye). Avoid getting the piece too wet at the edges, as water may creep underneath into the unfired enamel on the back; however, if you do not lift it before it dries, sufficient enamel will no doubt remain in place.

11. Lift onto the pad with the palette knife, fire, and stone the edges.

12. Repeat with a third coat on both sides, making good any shortfall on the back.

13. Adjust a brooch pin to lie snugly on the back and roughen, with a stone, the enamel underneath where it will be glued.

14. Fix it with an epoxy glue.

REPOUSSÉ PLAQUES

The church brass in relief shown in the photograph below was enamelled by raising the design in copper foil and sgraffitoing the lines in LF98 liquid flux (using this flux for greatest clarity). A plaque of this type should have a narrow border turned underneath for extra strength and probably not exceed 2 × 5½in (5 × 14cm) overall.

Repoussé interpretation of an ancient brass from Pitstone Church.

THREE-DIMENSIONAL PIECES

This is another option that can be pursued, but bear in mind that these pieces could be fragile. They are probably best planned in paper – do not be surprised by the amount of copper you need.

The copper is shaped by any means you like and usually has its first coats of enamel applied to the separate pieces before they are combined. The very thin copper wires from standard electrical cable are very useful for fixing pieces together for fusing, and for suspending them in the kiln for firing.

Hand-fashioned copper dishes.

A water lily night-light holder.

The water lily in the photograph above has four complete circlets of petals above a large leaf and is made strong enough for table use with several layers of enamel.

SIMPLE COPPER SHIM DISHES

These lightweight dishes are fashioned by hand in thin and soft copper foil with the aid of kitchen crockery, and finished in any transparent enamel that looks attractive when applied directly onto copper.

PROJECT – A COPPER DISH

1. Cut a disk from the foil, not more than 4in (10cm) across for firing in a U5 (or similar) kiln.
2. Bend its sides up by pressing them into the curve of a saucer and working round the disk (this will develop a much smaller and deeper dish than the saucer). Check that its rim is level by turning it over on a flat surface.
3. Select a slightly deeper bowl, possibly a pudding plate, and bend up the sides further in the same way, trying to create many small crinkles rather than large folds.
4. Finally, if you want a deeper bowl, repeat in a steeper-sided pudding bowl – use one with dimensions bigger than the intended dish and mould its curved side against the part of the bowl where it bends most. Check the rim is level and adjust the shape until you are satisfied.

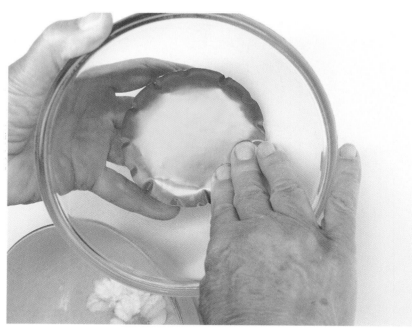

Shaping the copper in a pudding basin.

soft white on top of the unfired transparent enamel.

- The amber dish was given its shape by inducing the dozen folds regularly round the circumference while holding the centre flat with an upturned glass.

A more regular, flat-bottomed dish.

5. Pickle and clean thoroughly.
6. Put enamel on the inside by the gum, sprinkle and spray method, making sure you cover all the exposed copper evenly by rotating and slanting the dish, but avoid laying an over-thick layer.
7. Dry and fire on a mesh.
8. Pickle and clean the outside and enamel this in the same way. If you use a slightly distorted mesh it will only touch the rim of the upturned dish in a few places.

Notes on the above:

- It is possible to fire both sides together if you handle it carefully as you sprinkle the inside, turn it over then cover the outside. A large kitchen palette knife makes it easier to move while only touching the copper edges.
- The metallic look to some colours was achieved by a final thin sifting of

THE ARTISTIC IMPACT OF YOUR ENAMELS

Enamelling is fun! Learning to use the techniques described in this book should have been an enjoyable challenge. However, mastering the necessary skills really needs to be complemented by the artistry to capitalize on the unique qualities of the medium. Some appreciation of the age-old principles, common to all visual art, is an asset; they need not be followed slavishly, but do give thought to a piece's design and composition. For instance:

- Does the finished enamel have a balanced appearance?
- What impact do you want from the overall effect?
- Have you considered a focal point of interest?

A Small Tray

The flat bottom will need to be heavily indented with a design or lettering to give it strength and avoid warping. The edge can be crimped up with tweezers.

The one illustrated was an experiment, enamelled with LF98 liquid flux and sgraffitoed on top of the raised lettering. This thin coating of flux is lightweight enough for the piece, but other liquid enamels would probably be inappropriately heavy for these thin copper bowls.

A tray with a story to tell!

♦ Is its aim purely decorative, eye-catching or humorous?

♦ Do the colours blend and how will the light be reflected from them and the metal surfaces?

An enamel's success owes much to whether it achieves its intended technical and artistic aims, but it must also be practical and suitable for its purpose, be that as a piece of jewellery, a picture, an insert into another work or just a novelty item. With the knowledge you have acquired you should now be in a position to decide for yourself what you will find most fulfilling. Have fun.

The final chapter and the Gallery are included to give a taste of the range of ways enamelling has developed and what can be achieved. Enamelling needs *craftsmanship* but is definitely *the art of applying glass to metal*!

9 Other Enamelling Techniques

Enamelling techniques requiring specialized skills and facilities fall outside the scope of this book. However, a brief explanation of some of those frequently encountered seems appropriate. Many of these techniques are illustrated in the Gallery.

CLOISONNÉ

This traditional form of enamelling is probably one of the best known and is most often found in major pieces, precious jewellery or manufactured oriental items. Nevertheless, it can actually be explored in a simple way without much extra equipment.

The name comes from the French *cloison*, that describes the 'cells', formed by wires, that enclose coloured enamels while the wires themselves emphasize the lines of the design. In general, silver, copper or even brass wire is rolled flat, bent to shape and used on its edge. If this is fired on top of a lightly enamelled piece it will sink into the coating, fusing in place and leaving the wire standing like walls ready for further enamel to be added on either side. Successive firings of wet-laid grains are normally built up right to the top of the wires, after which the whole piece is stoned flat and polished, most frequently mechanically.

Flash-firing restores a gloss to the enamelled surface, level with the top edges of the embedded wires.

This is a slow process that needs considerable expertise, as well as involving the removal of all the firescale forming on the exposed wires each time the piece is fired. The technique is therefore more viable for craftsmen producing more valuable items by enamelling on silver or gold. They may also use specialized solder to fix the wires to the underlying metal in complicated designs.

Vitrum Signum (*see* Further Information) stocks some silver blanks and precious metal supplies. Cloisonné wire can be bought suitably milled to shape. The photograph below shows ways in which they can be used in this technique.

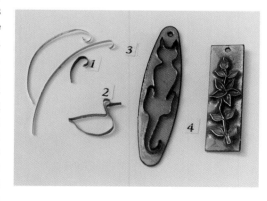

Some stages in cloisonné enamelling.

1. Milled wires. The silver wire can be safely fired onto enamelled silver or silver foil surfaces, but a copper base will present specific problems. Brass wire does not produce black firescales but is more springy to shape and cannot be fired repeatedly without the metal deteriorating. Copper is easy to manipulate but scales badly.

   The wire is best bent in the fingers and with specialized pliers or tweezers. It needs to stand snugly on the base enamel, but wires can be gently pushed down into the molten enamel with a palette knife.

2. The bird is shaped with a single wire, although more complicated patterns will involve many pieces of wire. Bends make them easy to place and the enclosed areas for the enamel are formed with the carefully planned introduction of further wires.

3. The top and bottom of the cat are bent separately and join inside the hips. It was held in place on the base with gum before being fired. The firescale must be removed from the wires before a black cat, blue sky and the wall are added in wet-laid enamels.

4. This test piece has a more complex design with each flower formed using two wires and most leaves bent separately. It also illustrates the concave effect of the enamel surface when the cells are only partially filled (with two layers), sometimes known as Russian cloisonné.

The puppy has brass wire on a copper base; the bird has silver wire over a base covered with silver foil. Both were enamelled to the top of the wires, stoned flat and flash fired. (*See also* Gallery pictures 19–24.)

Above: silver cloisonné pendants made with only simple tools.

Two boxes with cloisonné insets.

CHAMPLÊVÉ

Traditionally, engraving tools are used to dig out cells, leaving the essence of the design proud. This is left uncovered by enamel, while the engraved (sunken) areas are filled. These are the 'raised fields' of enamel in the French term *champlêvé*.

In modern enamelling the metal is frequently etched or photo-etched away; alternatively, castings can be used. (*See also* Gallery pictures 24–29 and 33–34.)

PLIQUE-Á-JOUR

Transparent enamels are fused and left without any backing in a lattice of open metal cells to give a 'stained glass window' effect. Small cells can be filled purely by wet-laying; larger pieces are enamelled on a copper former that is subsequently etched away with acid. (*See also* Gallery pictures 30–31.)

BASSE-TAILLE

This is a term describing the technique of varying the depth of transparent enamels by engraving or indenting the underlying metal by any means. The resultant changes in the density of colour give the design added form or emphasis, as can be seen in Gallery pictures 15, 24–25, 28–29 and 32.

GRISAILLE

A specialized monochrome development of painting enamelling, usually white over a black base. The densest white is built up in several coats. (*See* Gallery picture 12.)

Gallery

This Gallery is designed to show a wide range of the enamelling currently being produced in the UK by enamellers ranging from professionals of international repute to the far less experienced amateur. The earlier ones use techniques introduced in this book; the later require more specialized advanced workmanship. They illustrate some of the skill and artistry being shown by today's enamellers.

1. 'Blue Poppies' – sprinkled stencil on copper. Betty Butler

3. 'Dancing Figures' – stencil on copper. Julie Higgins

2. 'Shallow Water' – stencil, high fire, silver foil on copper. Betty Butler

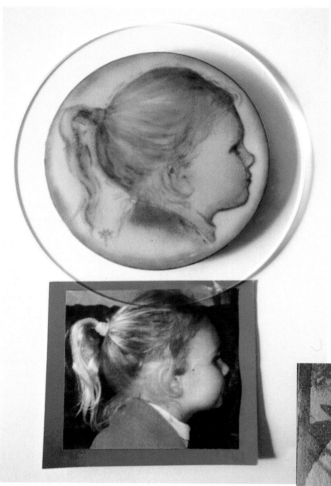

4. 'Portrait of a Girl' – stencil and painting on copper, worked from a photograph. May Yarker

5. 'Dance of the Spirit' – stencil and foil on copper. May Yarker

6. 'We're Looking at You' – wet-laid on copper. Joan Bolton King

7. 'Big Ben' – picture on copper. Harry Morley

8. 'Autumn Gold' – freeform brooch, swirling on copper. Kathleen Kay

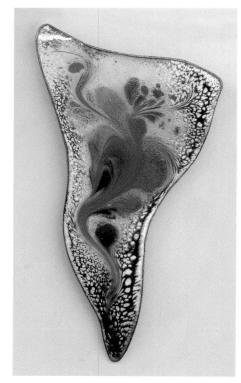

9. 'Screened Images Windows #10' – multi-technique using riso-screen printing, on copper with silver foil. Tina Cartledge

10. 'Tiggy' – painted enamel miniature on copper. Doreen Jenkinson

11. 'Woman Bathing in a Stream' (after Rembrandt) – painted enamel miniature. Doreen Jenkinson

12. 'The Apprentice Golfer' – grisaille. Janet Lamey

13. 'Abstract Design' –
sgraffito on 14in steel dish.
Richard Casey

14. 'Market Day, Northern
Town' (after L. S. Lowry)
– engraved enamel on
steel. Richard Casey

15. 'Maternity Mission' – repoussé with silver foil. Joan Bolton King

16. Pleated Bowl – torch-fired sprinkled enamel on thin copper. Maureen Carswell

17. Cross in St. Barnabas Church, Purley (2.5m high). Leslie Miller

18. Assembling the 63 copper with silver foil panels in the cross. Leslie Miller

19. Crab box lid – cloisonné on copper. Margery Levy

20. 'Cretan Dolphins' – cloisonné, silver wire on copper. Joan Bolton King

21. 'Tabby Sleeping' – cloisonné in fine gold and silver wire. Bonnie Mackintosh

22. 'Blowing a Kiss' – miniature whistle in silver cloisonné. Penny Gildea

23. Necklace – silver beads, gold wire cloisonné and malachite stones. Dorothy Budd

24. Snowdrops box lid –
cloisonné and champlevé
on silver. Gerald Lomax

25. Kingfisher brooch –
champlevé on silver. Gerald
Lomax

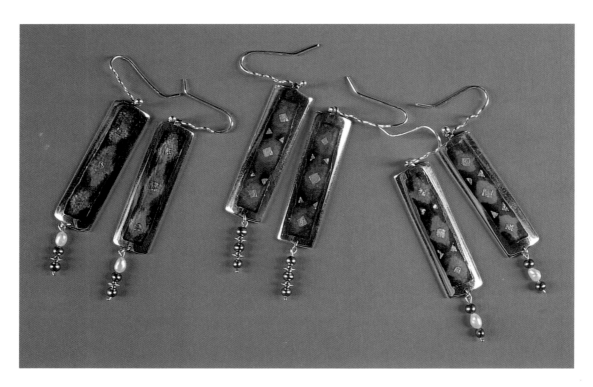

26. Earrings – with gold paillons inset, on silver. Linda Connelly (photograph: Ann Pethers)

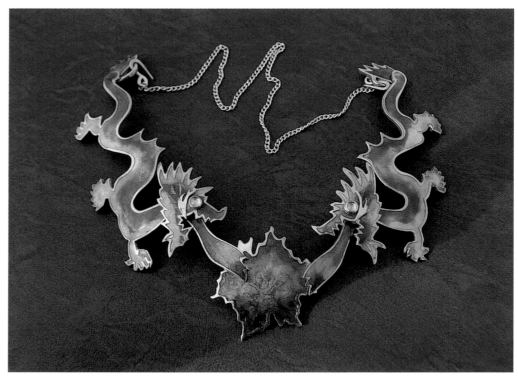

27. Dragon Necklace – champlevé on silver with gold foil and gold-plated edges. Dorothy Cockrell

28. Pendant – blue moonstone set in champlevé on gold. Sarah Wilson (photograph: Peter White)

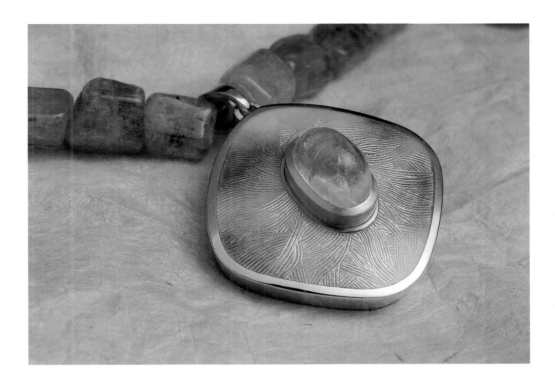

29. 'Fossils' – Armada dish, champlevé on silver. Sarah Wilson (photograph: Peter White)

30. Goblet (6in diameter) – plique-á-jour in silver. Dorothy Budd

31. Dragonfly brooches – plique-á-jour, silver and gold. K. Hali Baykov

33. 'Sculptured Object' – champlevé on silver. Jane Short (photograph: Robert Sanderson)

32. Rose necklace – silver and gold with peridot stones. K. Hali Baykov

34. 'Feather' vase from The
Worshipful Company of
Goldsmiths Collection –
champlevé on silver.
Jane Short

Further Information

BOOK LIST

Many books have been published on enamelling in the UK and USA but some are difficult to obtain, except from an enamelling guild or society members' library. The following selection has been made with consideration to those currently in print or available through County Libraries in the UK (where their Dewey decimal classification is 738/739). Search also under the American spelling, 'enameling'.

Clark, G., and Feher, F. and I., *The Technique of Enamelling* (Batsford, revised edition 1984)

Ball, F., *Experimental Techniques in Enamelling* (Van Nostrand Reinhold, 1972)

Bates, K. F., *Enameling: Principles and Practice* (World Publishing Co., 1951)

McGrath, J., *First Steps in Enamelling* (Apple Press, 1994)

Palmer, D., *New Crafts – Enamelling* (Lorenz Books/Anness Press, 1998)

Seeler, E., *The Art of Enamelling* (Rheinholdt, 1969)

Speel, E., *Dictionary of Enamelling History and Techniques* (Ashcroft, 1998)

Speel, E., *Popular Enamelling* (Batsford, 1984)

Strosahl, J. and J. L., and Barnhart, C., *A Manual of Cloisonné and Champlevé Enamelling* (Thames and Hudson, 1982)

Theilade, K. and Collins, L. *Popular Crafts Guide to Enamelling* (Argus Books 1986)

USEFUL ADDRESSES

UK Suppliers

W. G. Ball Ltd
Anchor Road
Longton
Stoke-on-Trent
ST3 1JW
Tel: 01782 313956/312286
Fax: 01782 598148
E-Mail: sales@wgball.com
(lead free and liquid enamels, kilns and general supplies)

The Enamel Shop
Suppliers of Enamelling Equipment and Materials
Trethinna House
Altarnun
Launceston
PL15 7SY
Tel: 01566 880092
Fax: 01566 880093
(kits and millefiori beads)

Milton Bridge Ceramic Colours
Unit 9
Trent Trading Park
Botteslow Street
Hanley
Stoke-on-Trent
ST1 3NA
Tel: 01782 274229
Fax: 01782 281591
E-Mail: miltonbridge@cwcom.net
Website:
www.miltonbridge.memail.com
(enamels, kilns, kits and general
supplies)

Vitrum Signum
9a North Street
Clapham Old Town
London
SW4 0HN
Tel/Fax: 020 7627 0840
Website: www.vitrumsignum.co.uk
(enamels, kilns, kits and general
supplies)

J. Smiths Metal Centres
42–56 Tottenham Road
London
N1 4BZ
Tel: 020 7253 1277
Fax: 020 7254 9608
(copper)

Fred Aldous
37 Lever Street
Manchester 1
M1 1LW
Tel: 0161 236 2447
Fax: 0161 236 6075
E-Mail: aldus@btinternet.com
Website: www.fredaldous.co.uk
(copper foil and craft supplies)

ENAMELLING SOCIETIES

Contacts for details of membership and national enamelling information are given here. Many also produce informative newsletters and journals, and some organize tutorials.

United Kingdom

The Guild of Enamellers
10 Camellia Close
Tiverton
Devon
EX16 6TZ
Tel: 01884 255168
E-Mail: judymckellar@lineone.net
(for enamellers and all interested
persons)

The British Society of Enamellers
30 Kingston Square
London
W8 5HH
Tel: 020 7928 3600
(primarily for professional enamellers)

Australia

The Enamellers Association
Ann Thomson (secretary)
10 Onthonna Terrace
Umina
2257
NSW
Australia
Tel: 02 4342 3423

Canada

Canadian Enamallists Association
David Hustler (president)
1 Ojibway Avenue
Toronto
Ontario
M5J-2C9
Canada
Tel: 416 203 0962
E-Mail: laura.beard@sympatico.ca

Germany

Kunstverein Coburg
Hans Holbein Weg 10
96450 Coburg
Germany.
Tel: 9561 28285
E-Mail: edmund massow@surfeu.de
Website: mitglied.tripod.de/
KunstvereinColburg_2

India

The India Enamel Society
Veenu Shah
B-25 Chiragh Enclave
New Delhi – 110048
India
E-Mail: veenus@nde.vsnl.net.in

Israel

Enamel Section
Israel Design Craftsman's Association
Marga Michaeli
PO Box 17087
Tel-Aviv 61170
Israel
Tel/Fax: 972 3 6994657

USA

The Enamilist Society,
Barbara Minor (president)
PO Box 631704
Cincinnatti
Ohio 45263 1704
USA

Glass on Metal
Tom Ellis (editor)
PO Box 310
Newport
Kentucky 41072
USA
Tel: 859 291 3800
E-Mail: Tom Ellis thompson@rml.net or
Klindle@email.uc.edu
Website:
www.craftweb.com/org/enamel/enamel.
/htm

Index